COLORING BOOK FOR GIRLS

FASHION DESIGN

Sketchbook

FIGURE TEMPLATE

This book belongs to:

Niky Jadesson

FASHION

Niky Jadesson

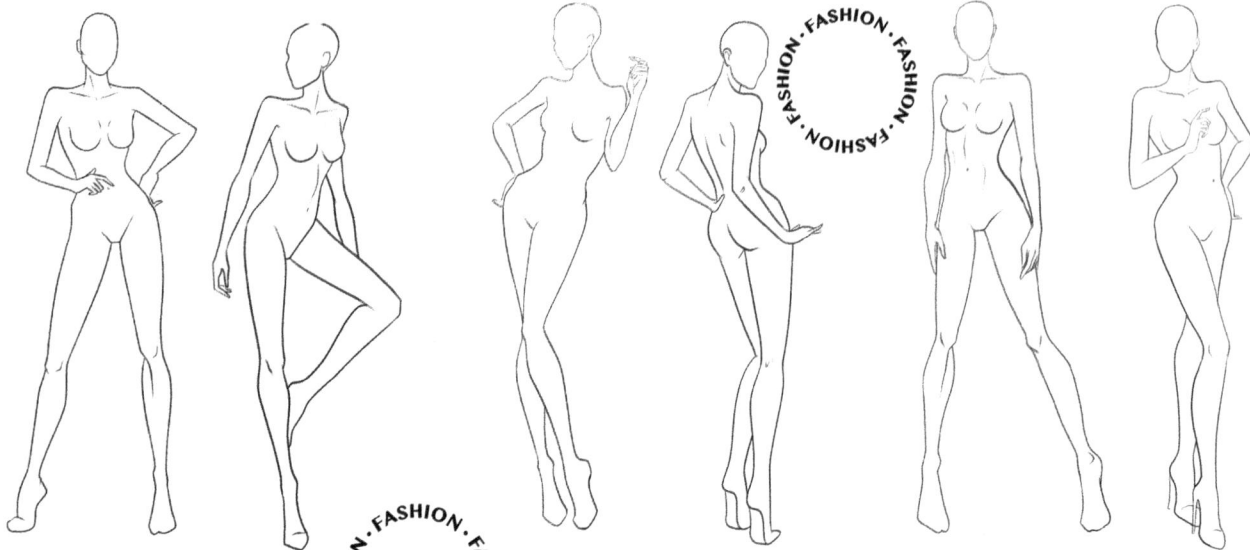

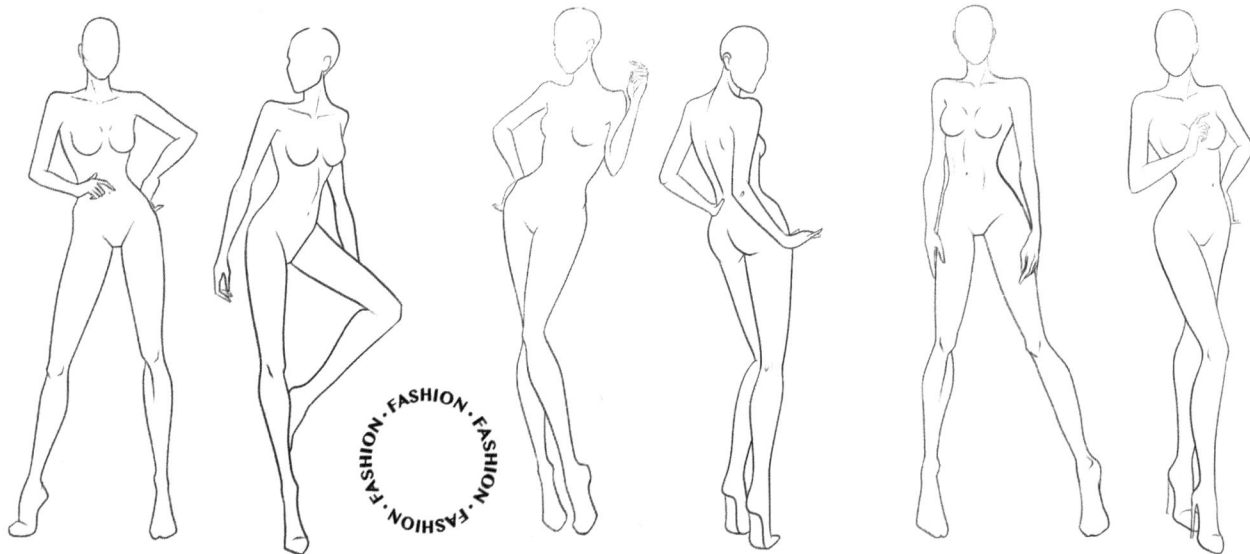

FASHION · FASHION · FASHION · FASHION ·

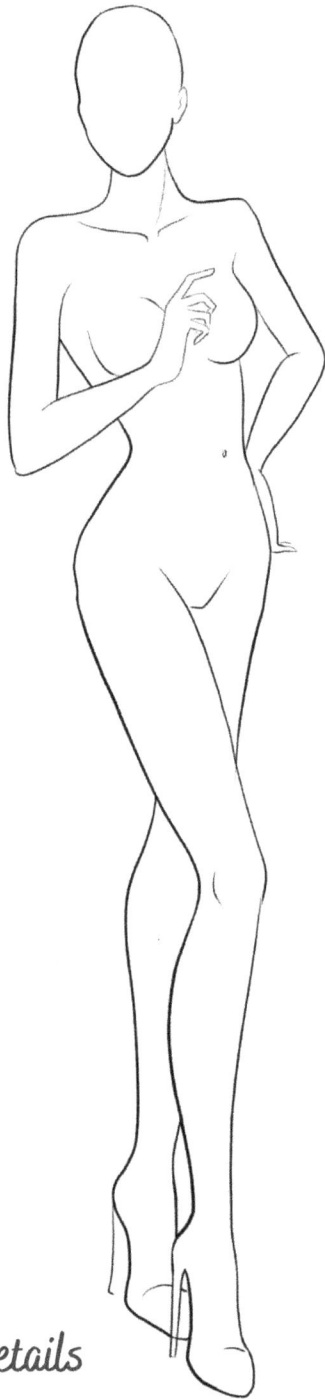

Trends

FASHION

Inspiration

Textiles

FASHION

Notes

Swatches

Details

FASHION   **FASHION**

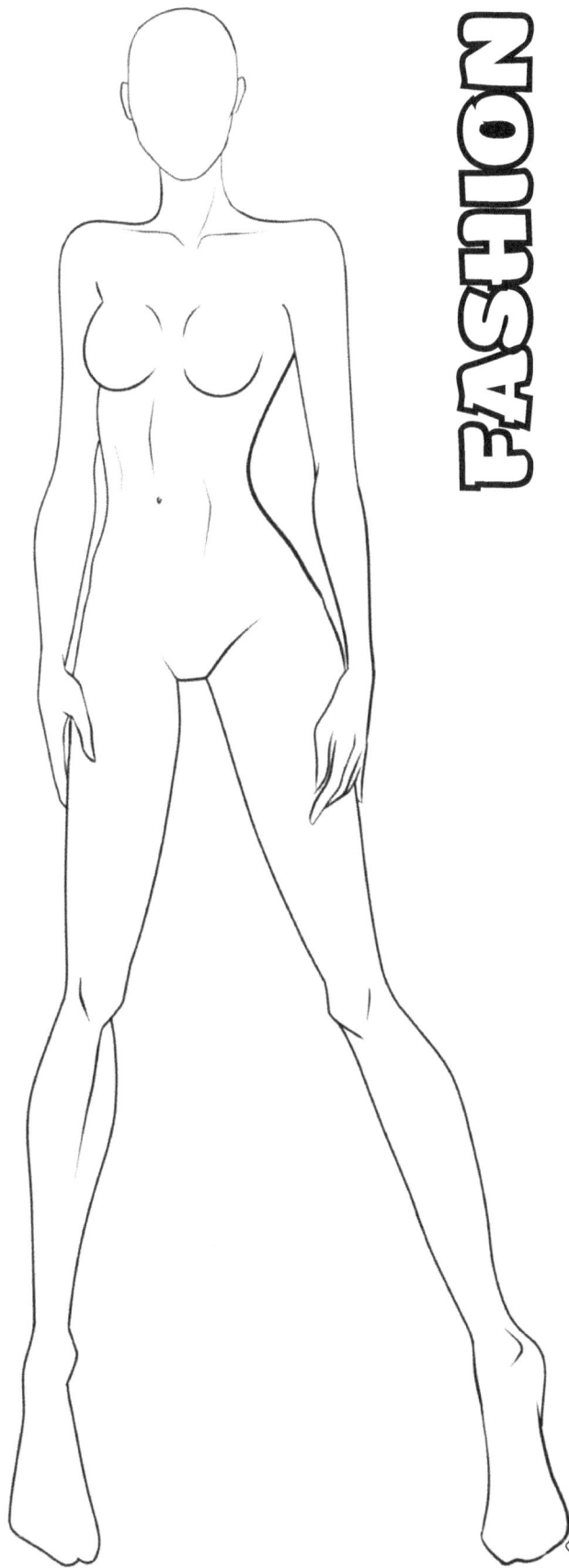

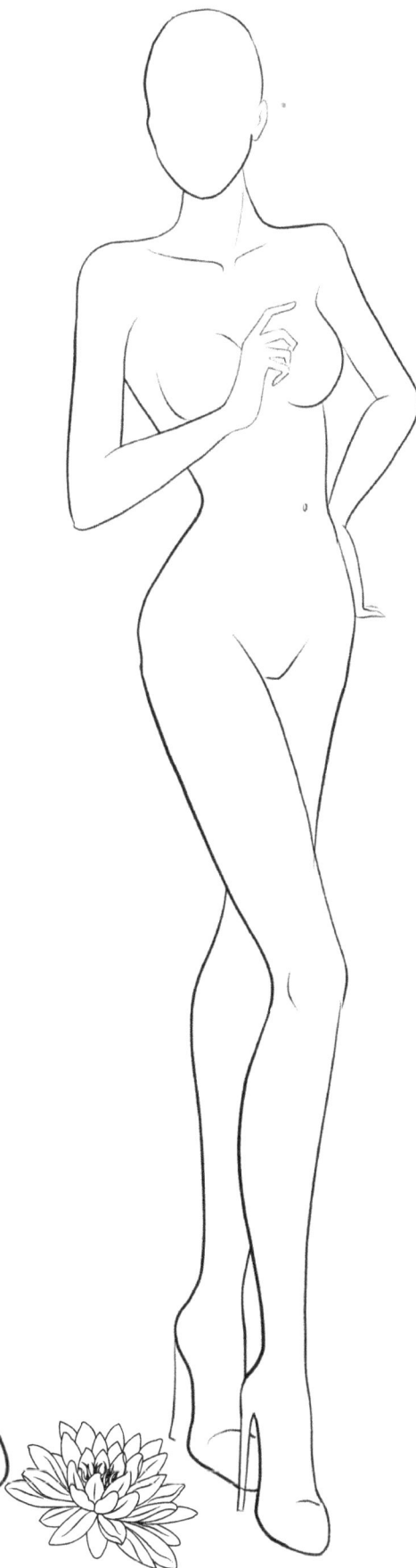

FASHION

FASHION

FASHION

STYLE · STYLE · STYLE · STYLE · STYLE · STYLE · STYLE

FASHION

Trends

_____
_____
_____

Inspiration

_____
_____
_____

FASHION

Textiles

_____
_____
_____

Notes

_____
_____
_____

Swatches

Details

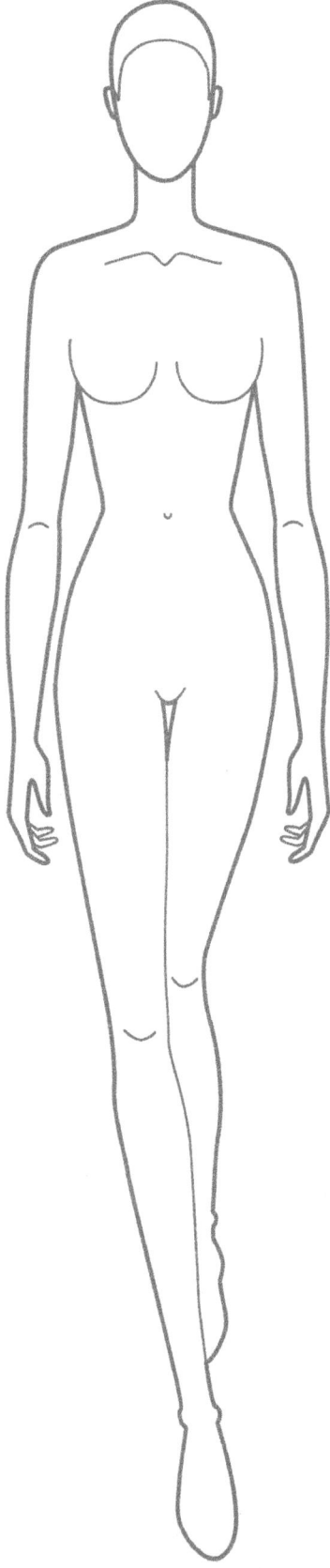

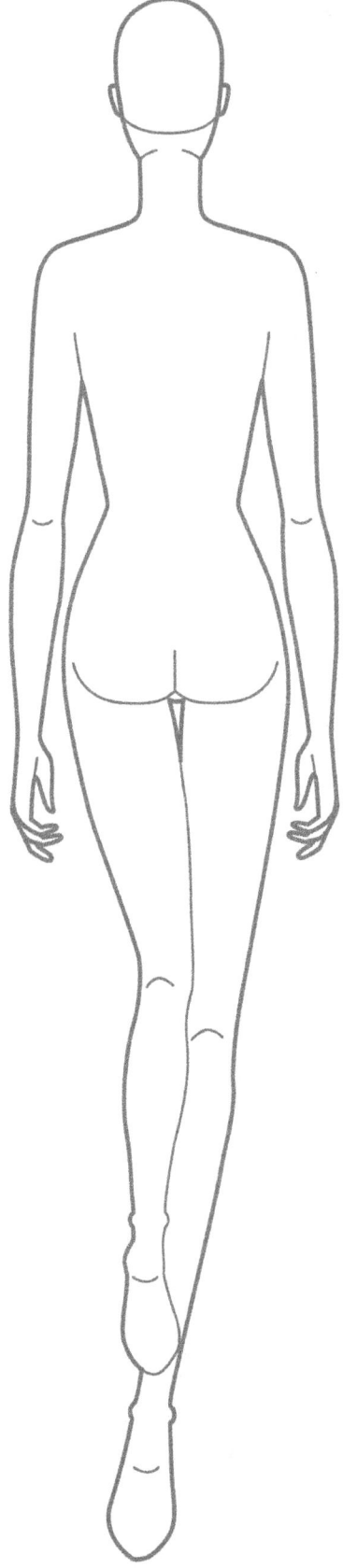

FASHION

FASHION

Trends

_____

_____

_____

Inspiration

_____

_____

_____

Textiles

_____

_____

_____

Notes

_____

_____

_____

_____

Details

Swatches

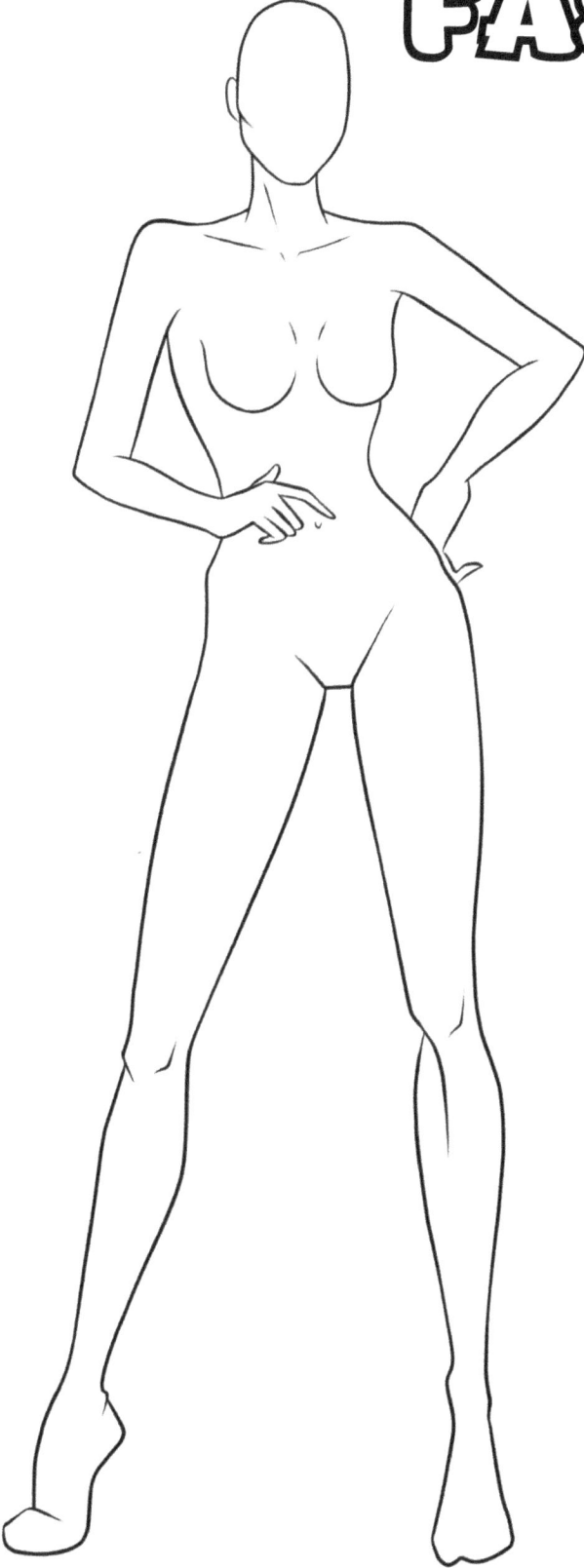

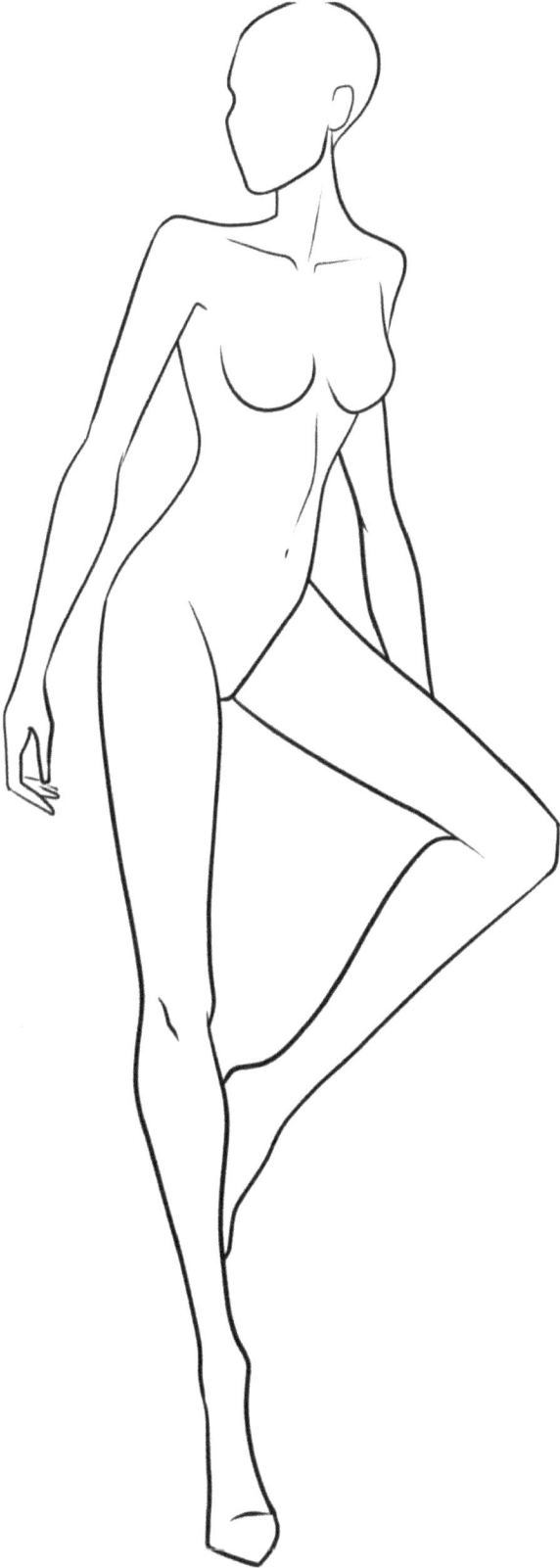

FASHION

FASHION

FASHION

Trends

FASHION

Inspiration

Textiles **FASHION**

Notes

Swatches

Details

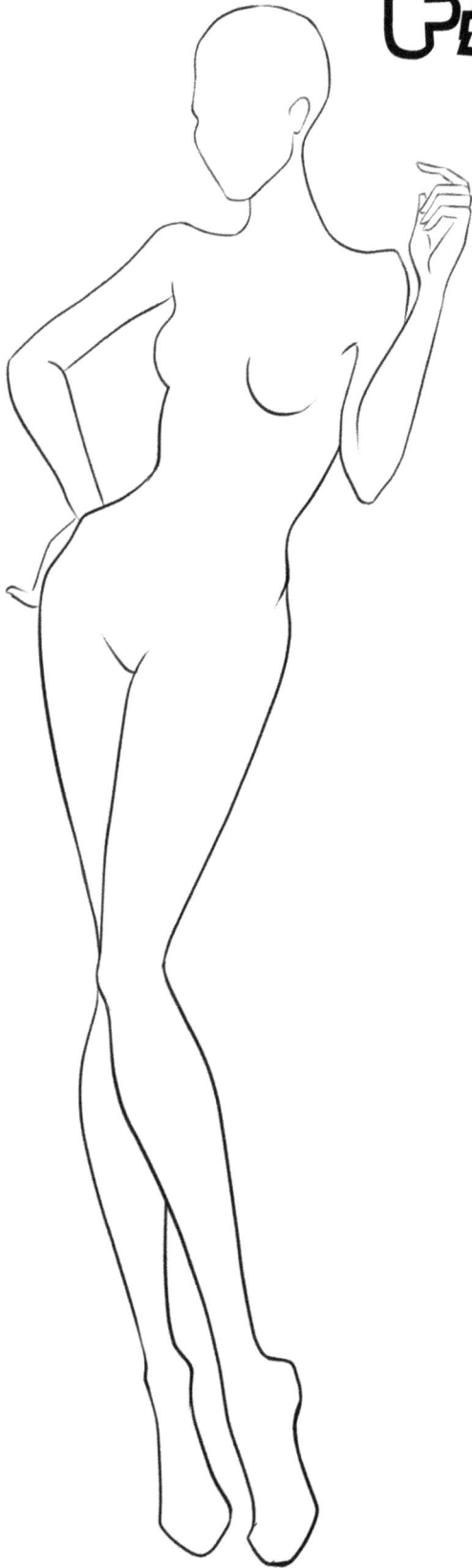

FASHION

FASHION

FASHION

STYLE · STYLE · STYLE · STYLE · STYLE · STYLE · STYLE · STYLE · STYLE

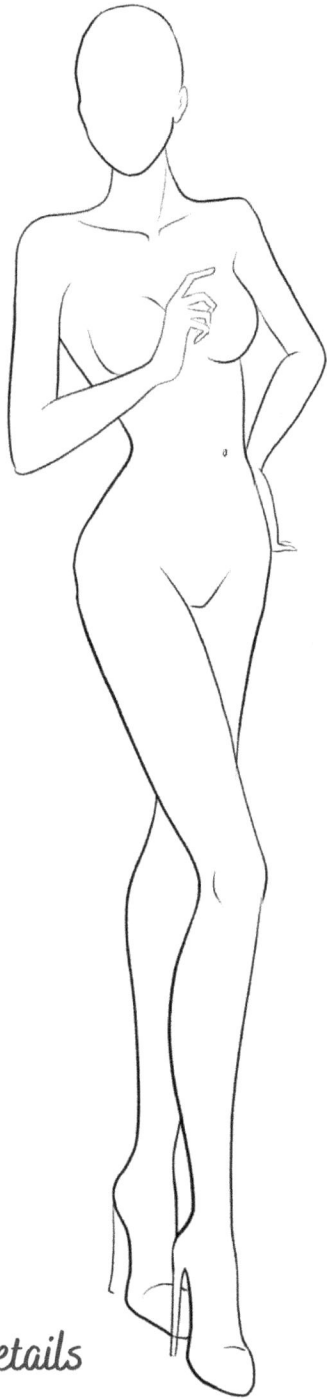

Trends
_____
_____
_____

Inspiration
_____
_____
_____

Textiles
_____
_____

Notes
_____
_____
_____

Swatches

Details

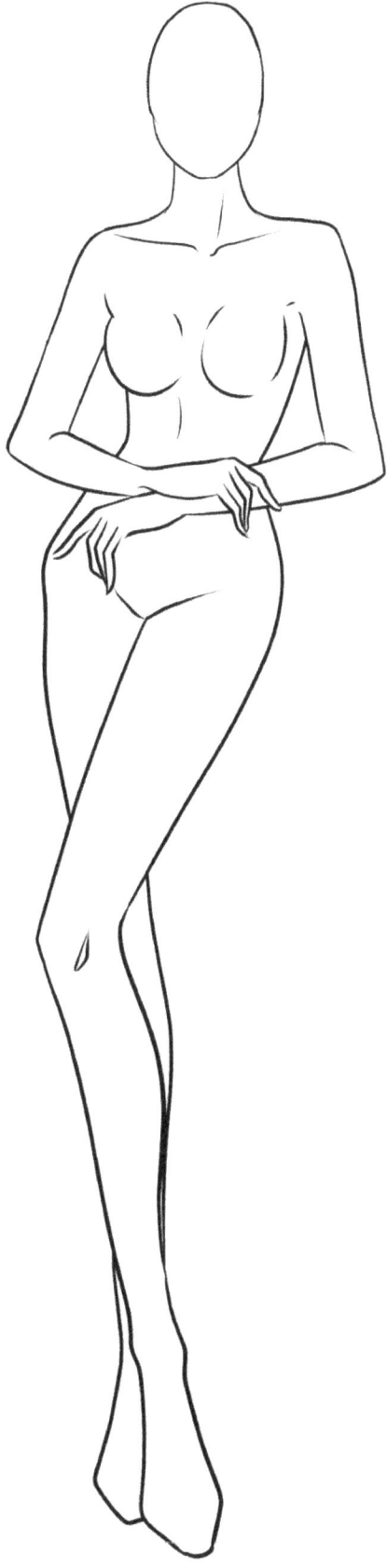

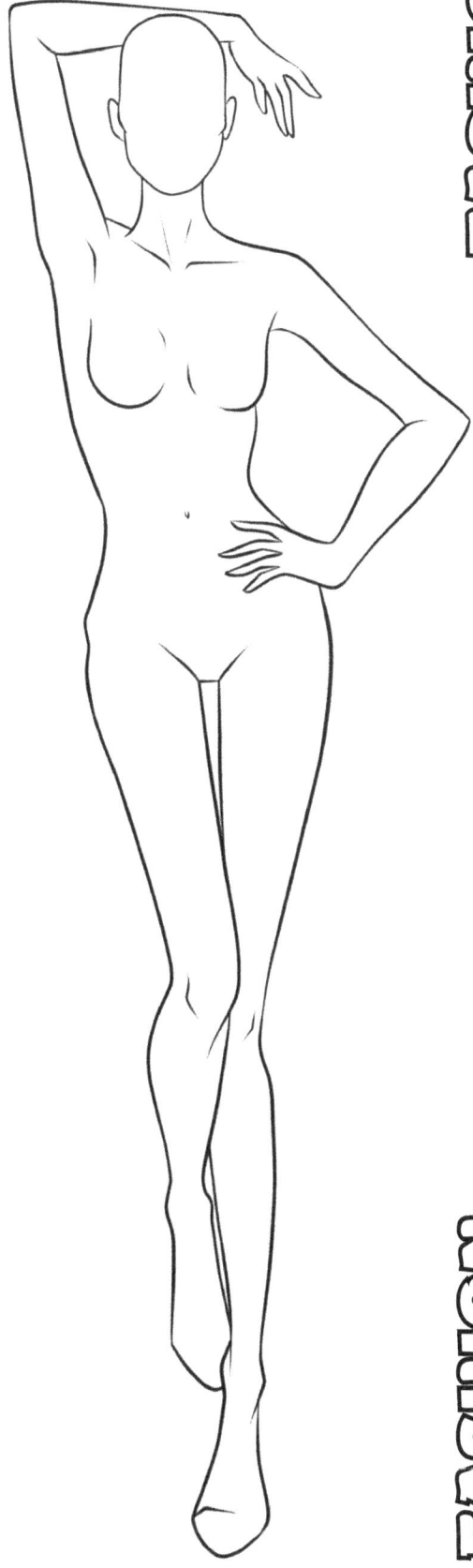

COLLECTION · COLLECTION · COLLECTION · COLLECTION ·

FASHION

Trends

_____

_____

Inspiration

_____

_____

_____

Textiles

_____

_____

_____

Notes

_____

_____

_____

Details

Swatches

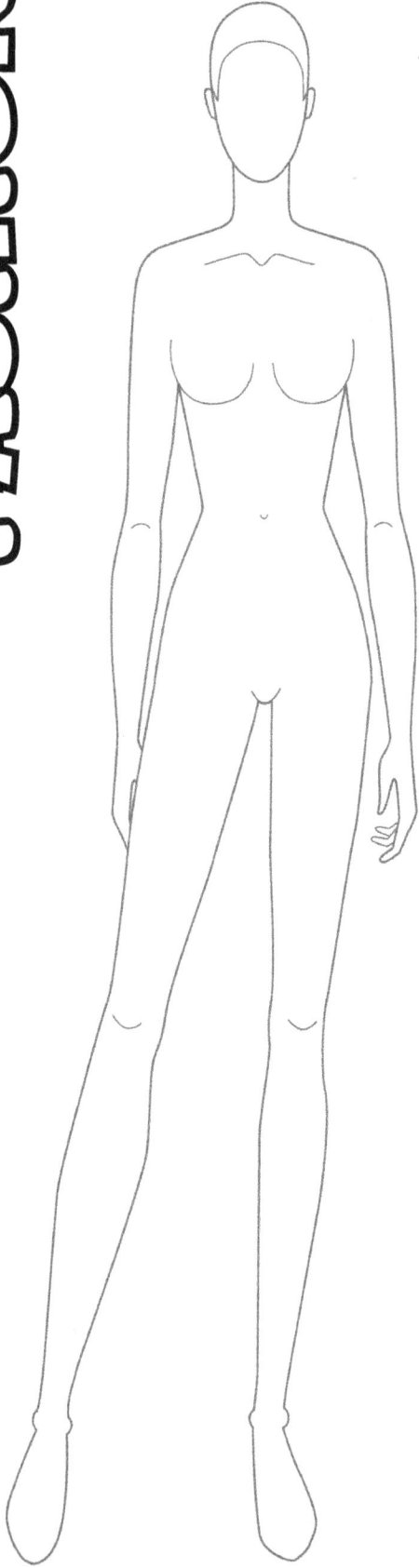

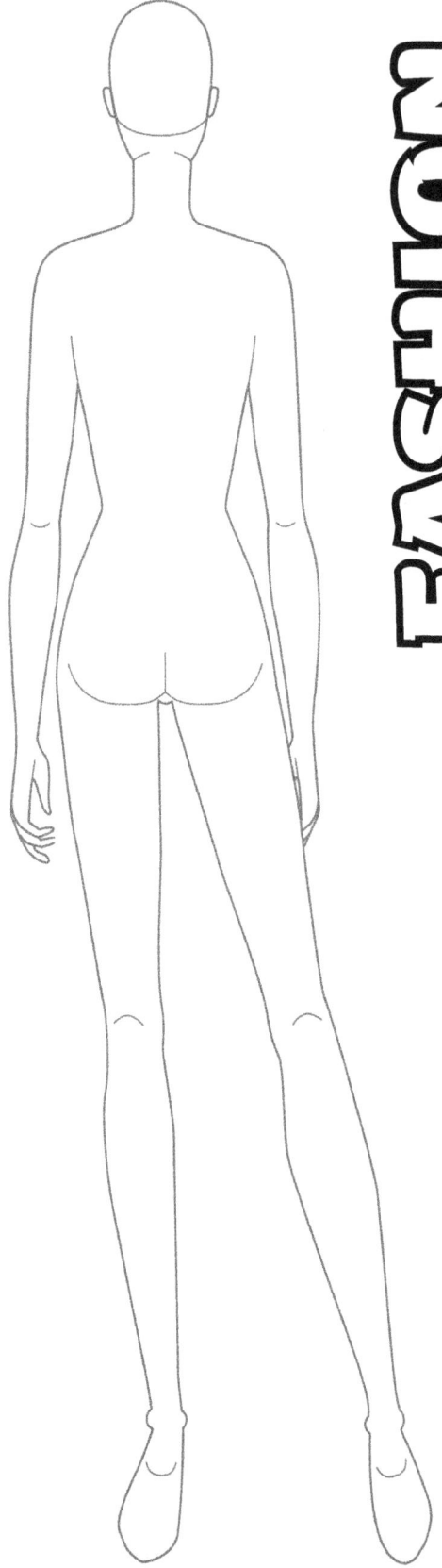

FASHION

FASHION

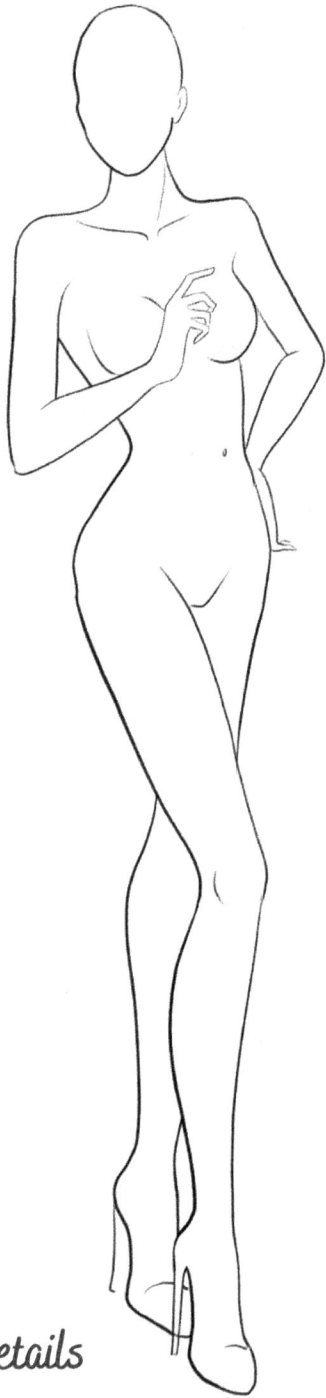

Trends

_____
_____
_____

Inspiration

_____
_____
_____
_____

Textiles

_____
_____
_____

Notes

_____
_____
_____

Swatches

Details

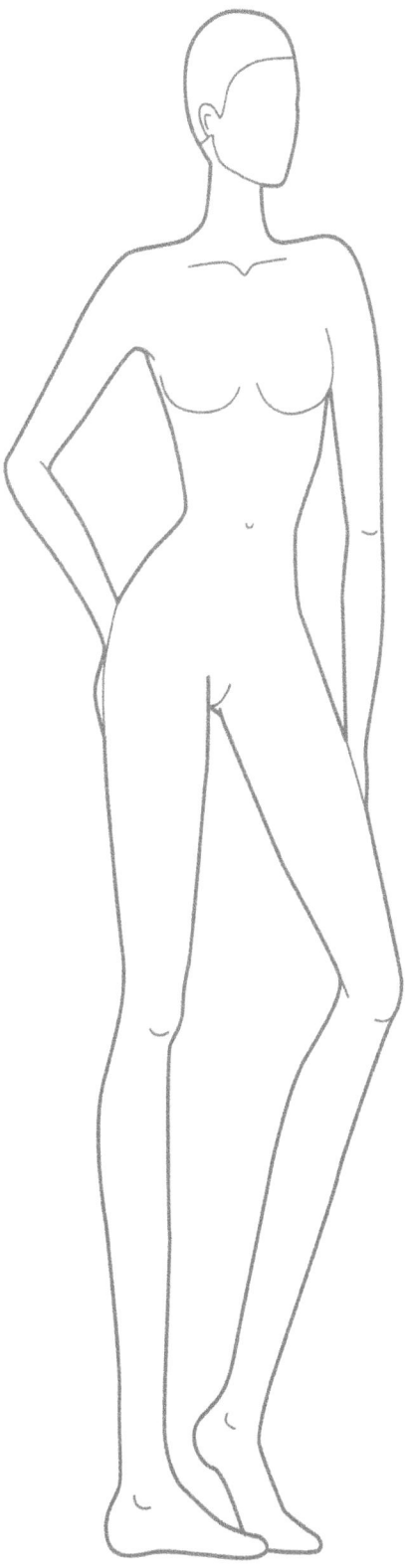

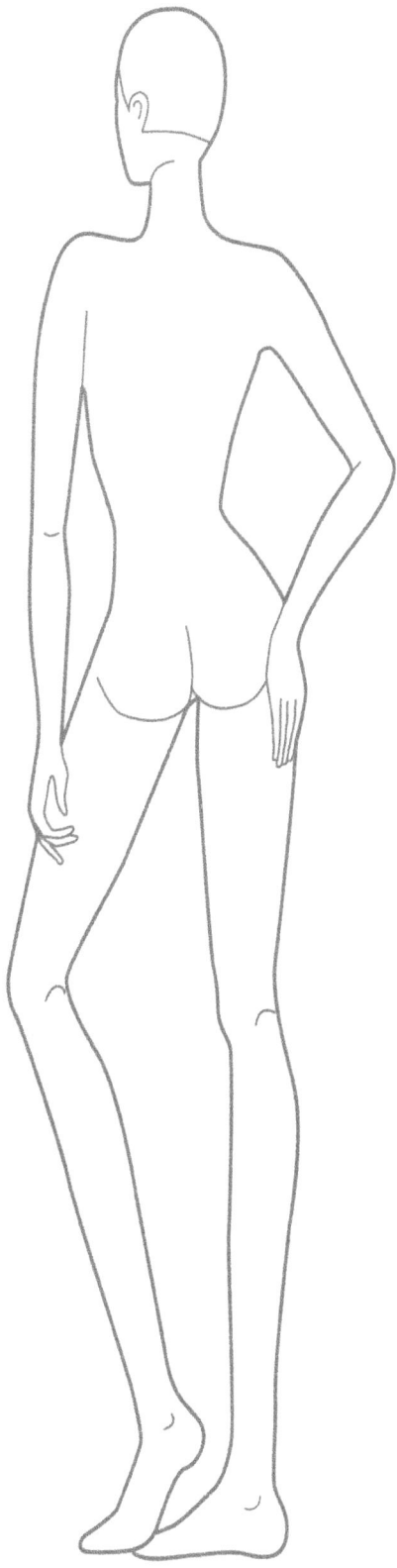

FASHION

FASHION

NEW · NEW · NEW · NEW · NEW · NEW · NEW · NEW

FASHION

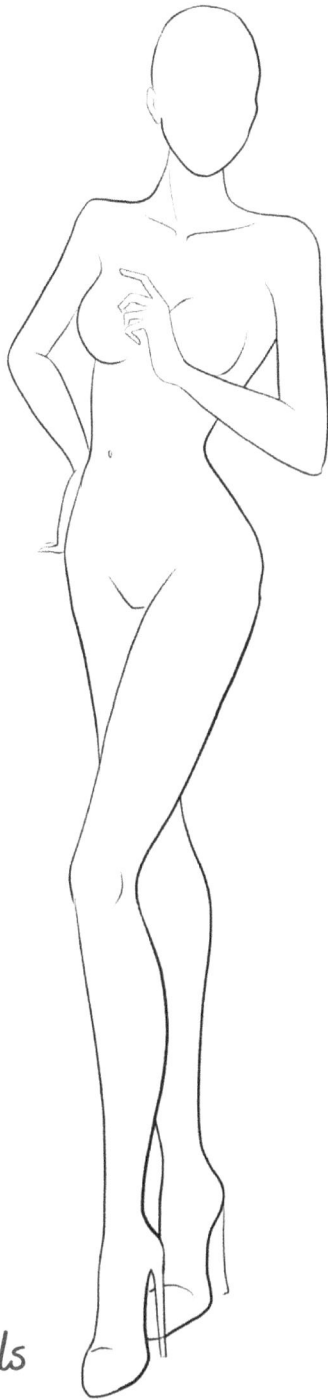

Trends FASHION

_____

_____

_____

Inspiration

_____

_____

Textiles FASHION

_____

_____

Notes

_____

_____

_____

Swatches

Details

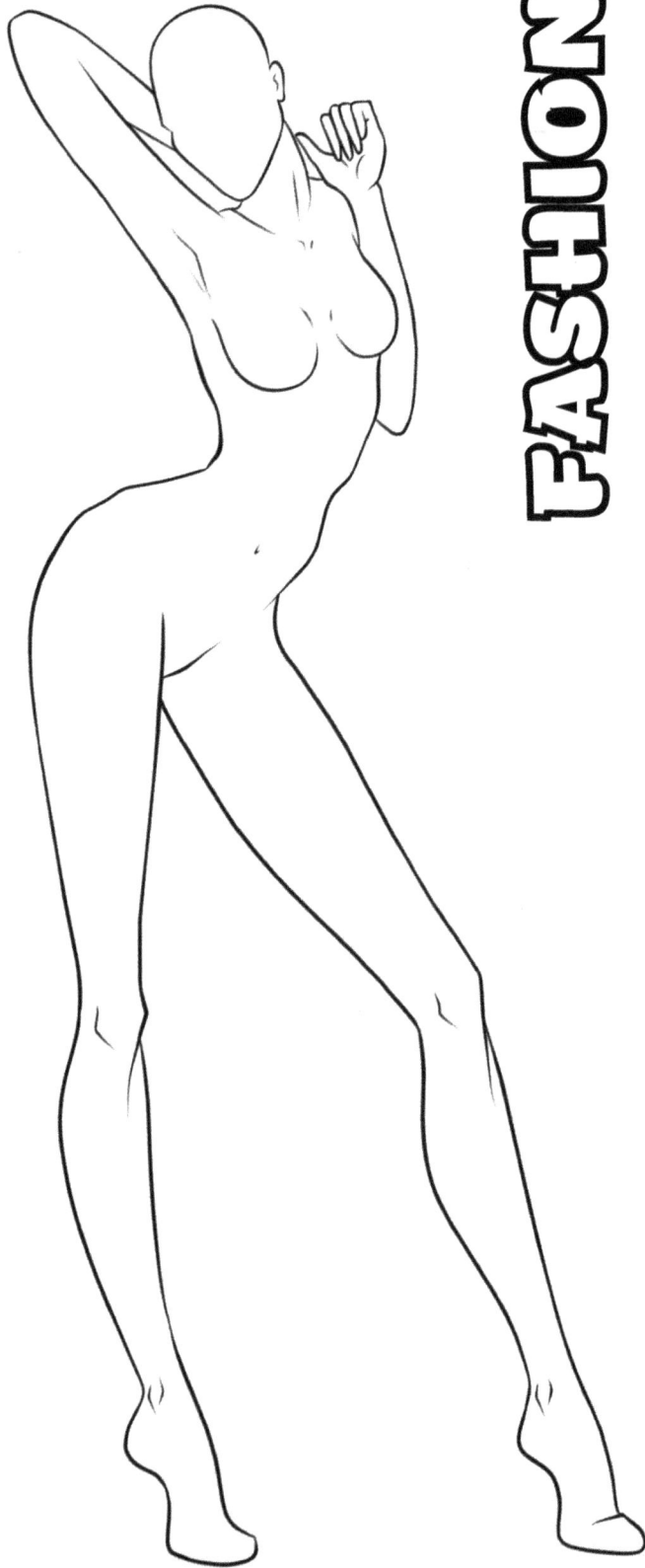

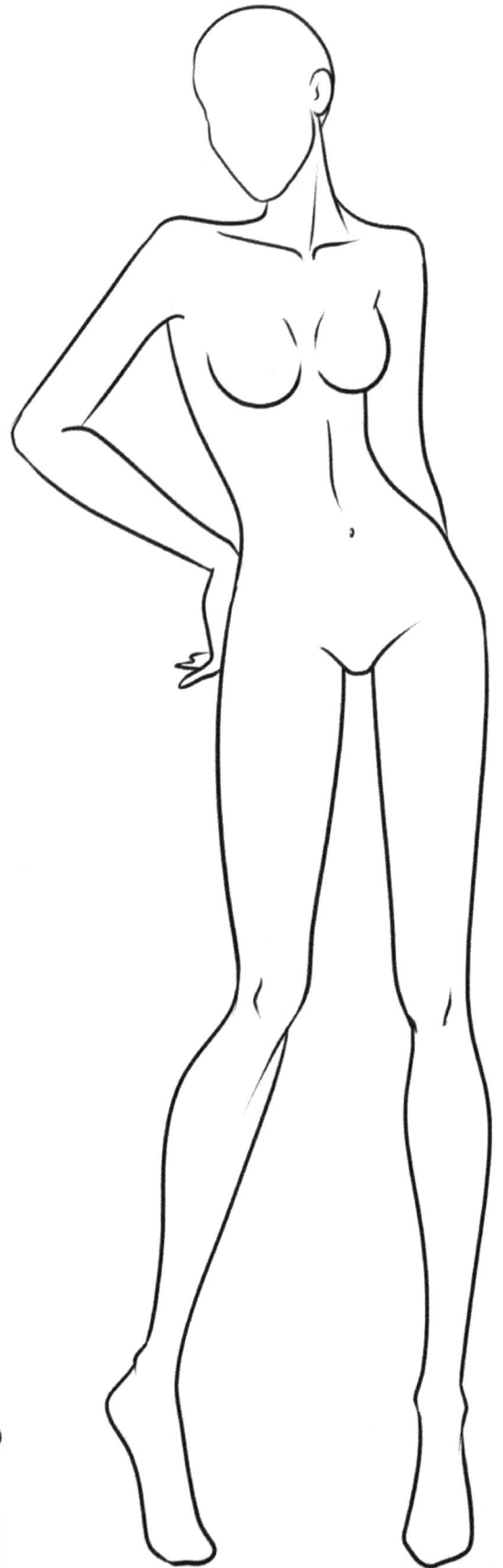

FASHION

FASHION

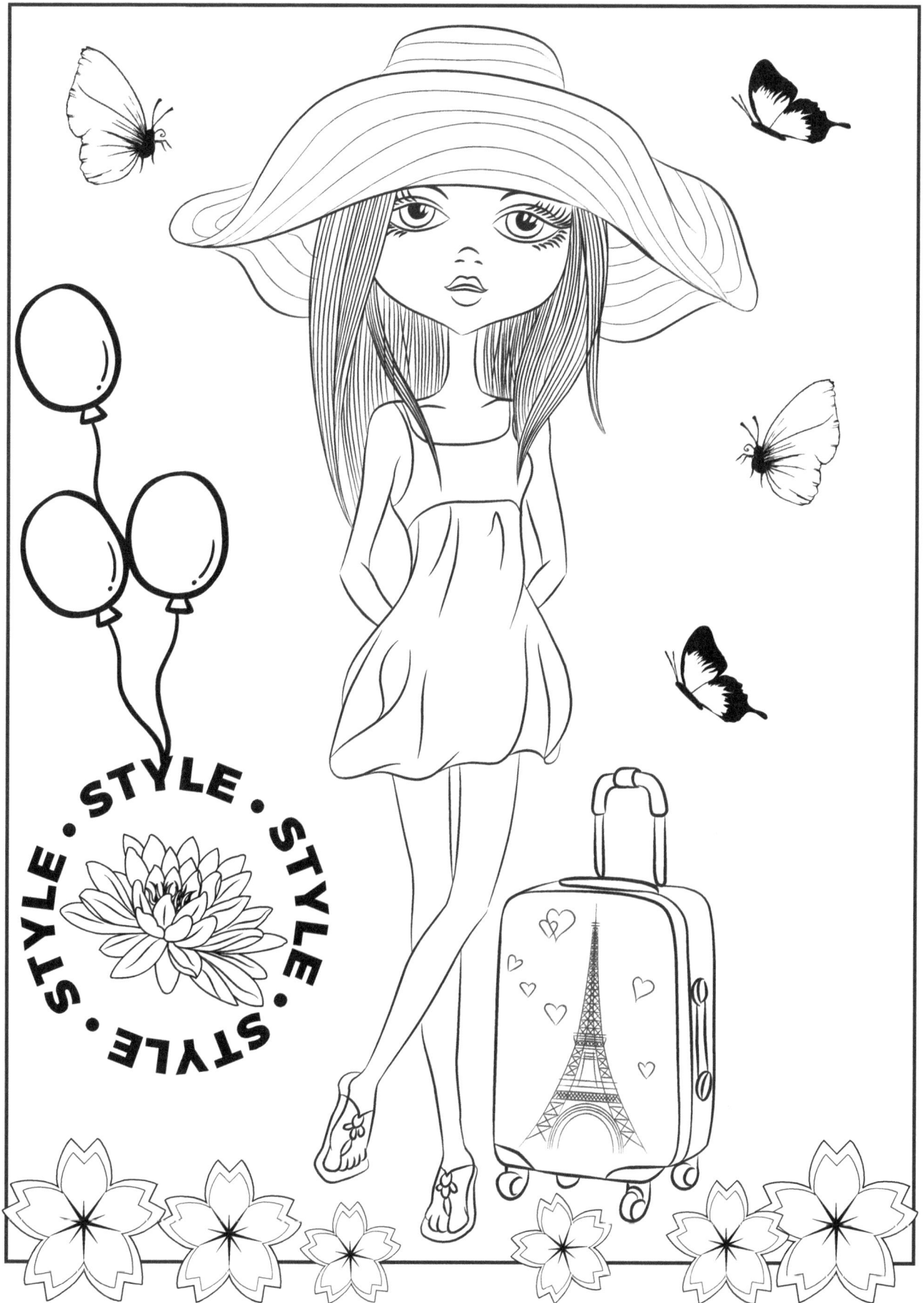

STYLE · STYLE · STYLE · STYLE · STYLE ·

Trends

FASH ✕ **ION**

Inspiration

Textiles

FASH ✕ **ION**

FASH ✕ **ION** Notes

Swatches

Details

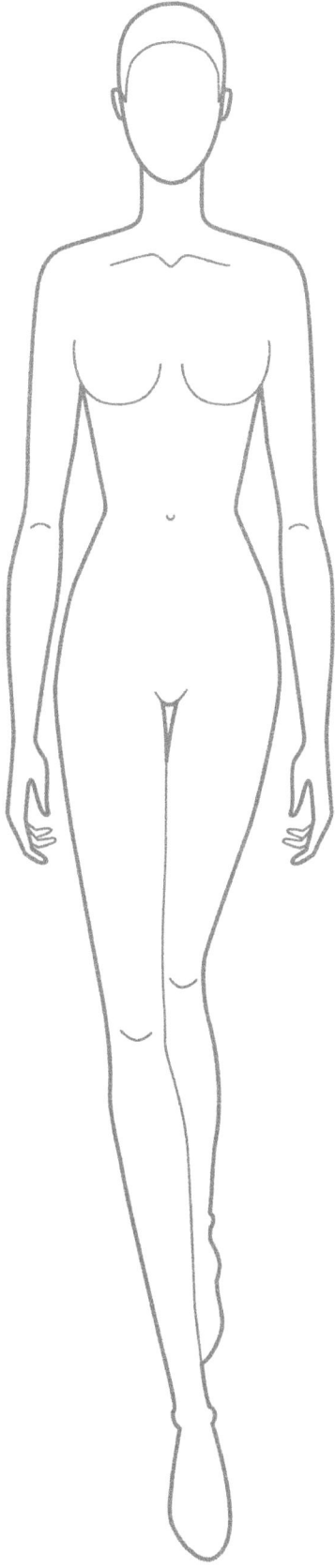

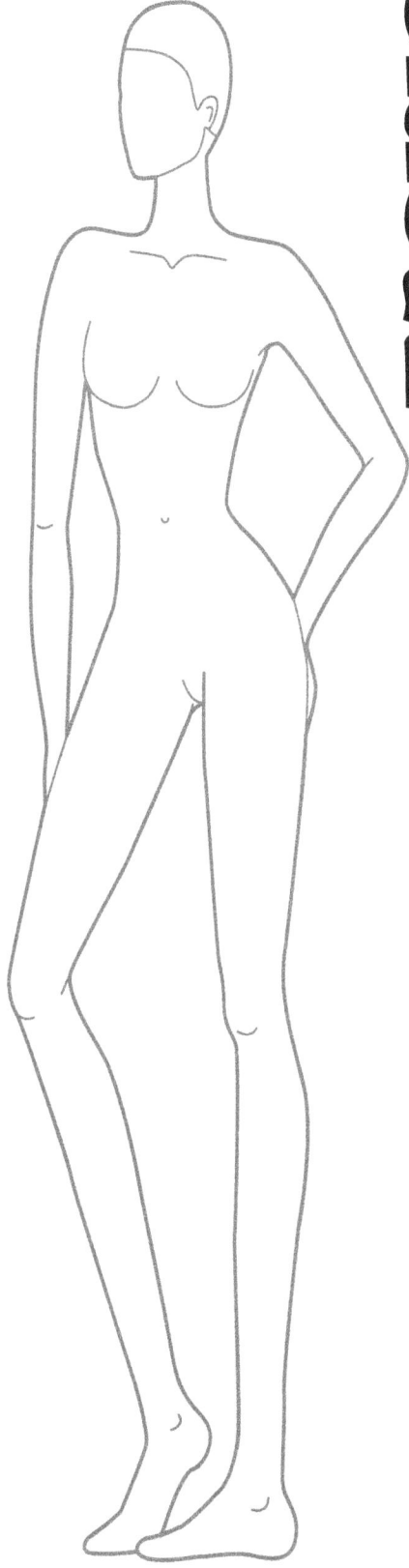

FASHION

FASHION

FASHION

Trends   **FASHION**

Inspiration

Textiles   **FASHION**

FASHION _Notes_

Swatches

Details

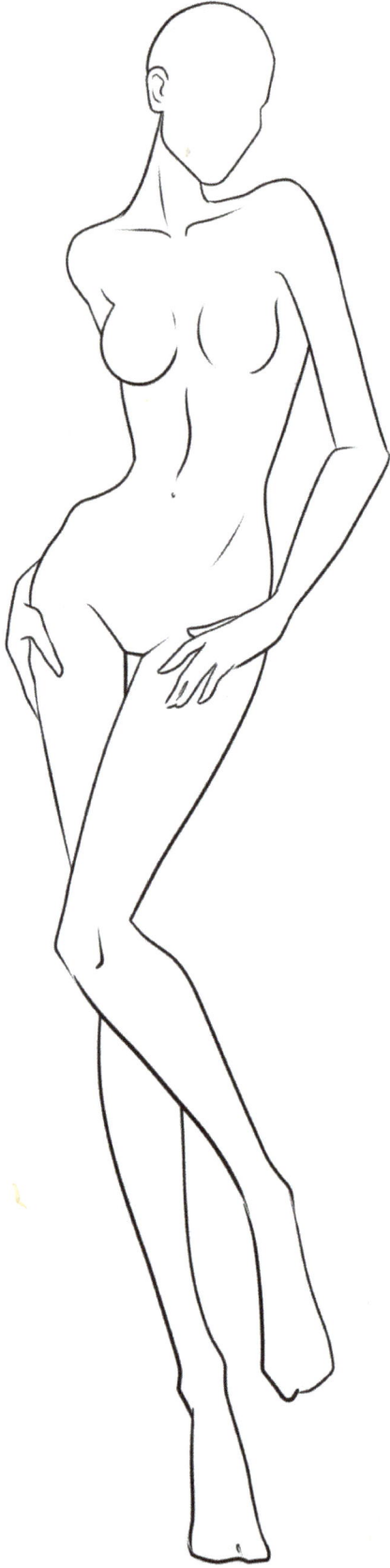

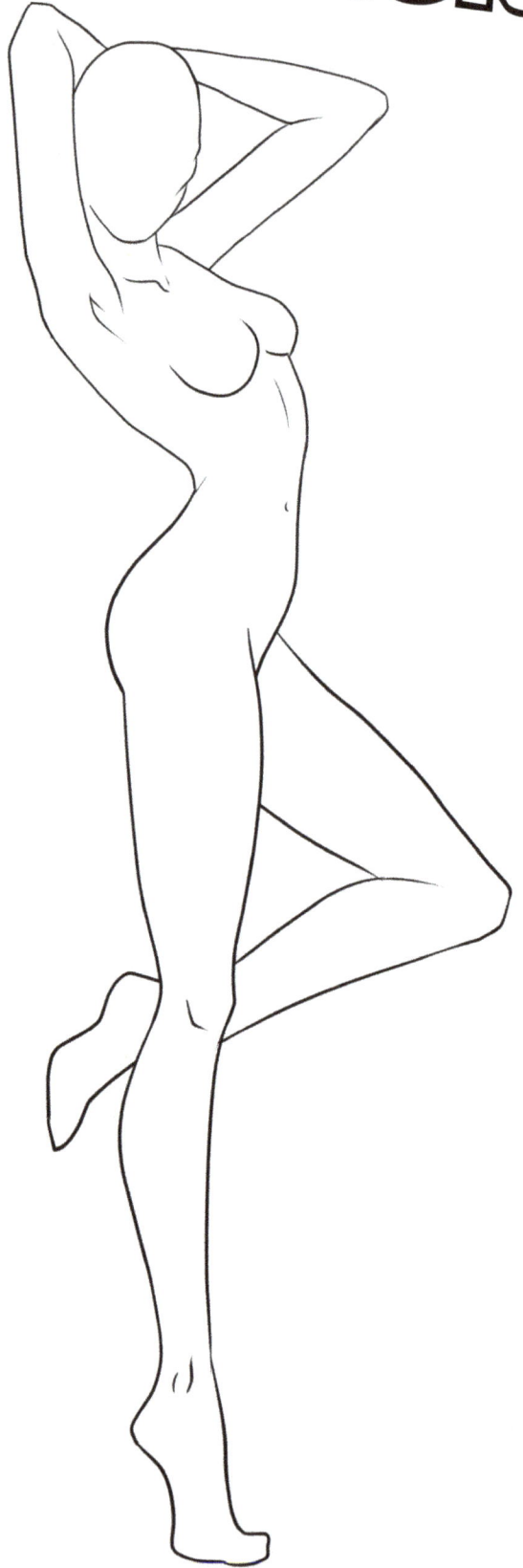

FASHION

FASHION

FASHION

FASHION · FASHION · FASHION · FASHION ·

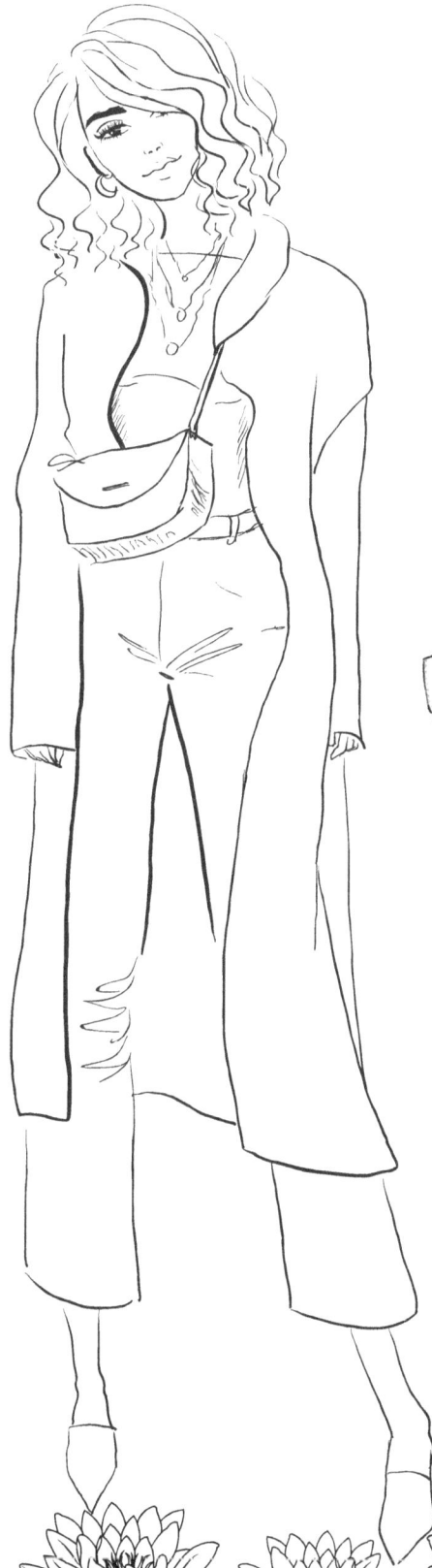

Trends   **FASHION**
_____
_____
_____

FASHION Inspiration
_____
_____
_____
_____

Textiles
_____
_____
_____

FASHION Notes
_____
_____
_____

Swatches

Details

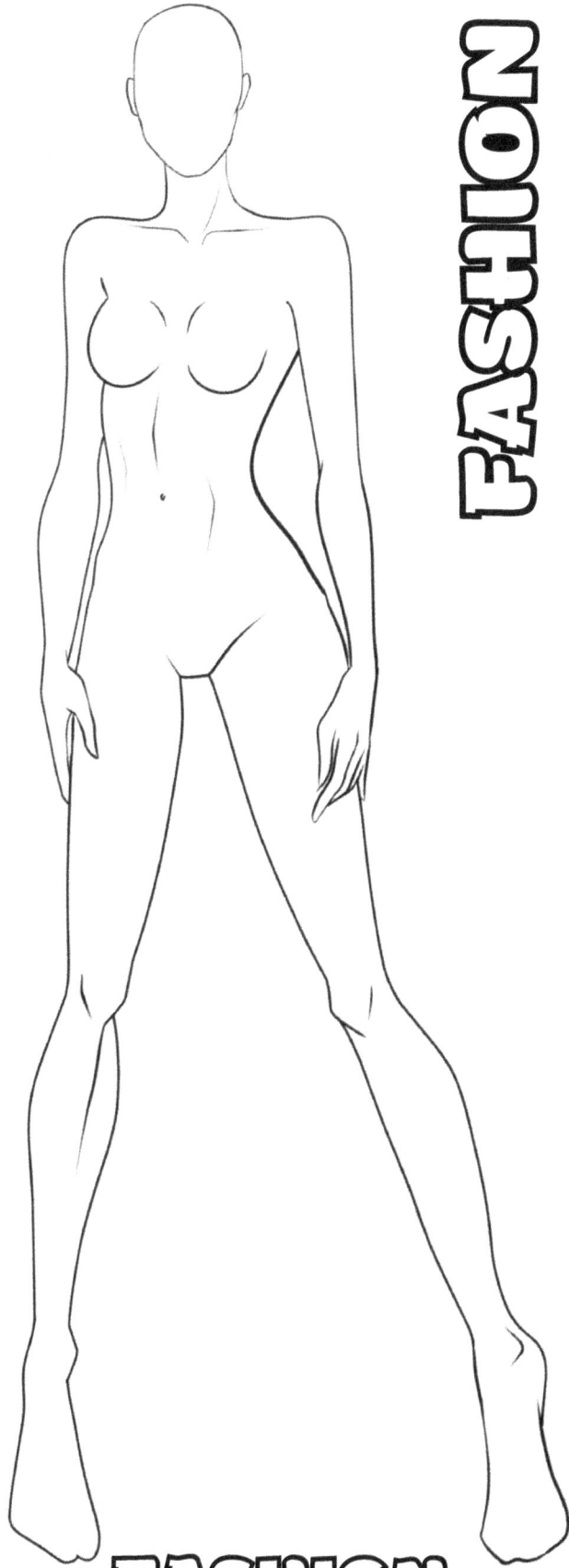

STYLE · STYLE · STYLE · STYLE · STYLE · STYLE ·

Trends

FASHION

Inspiration

Textiles

Notes

Swatches

Details

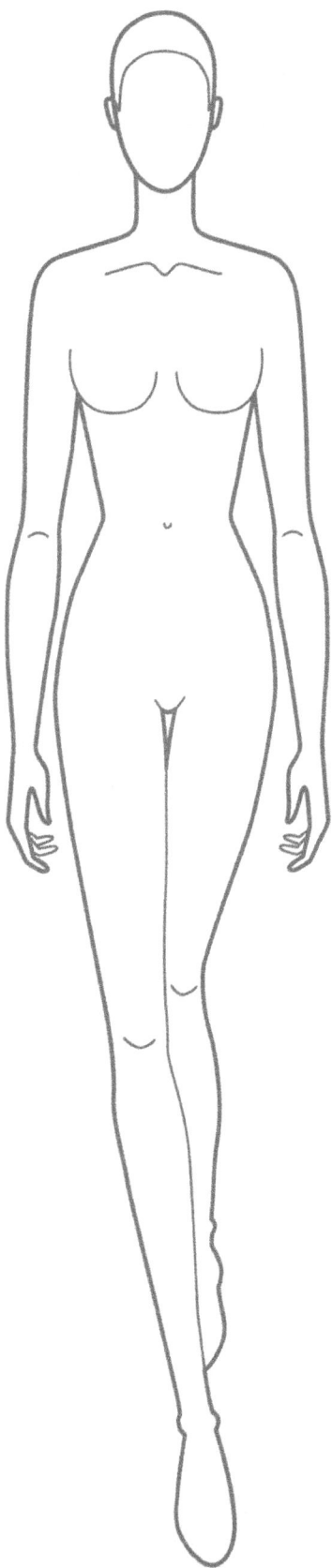

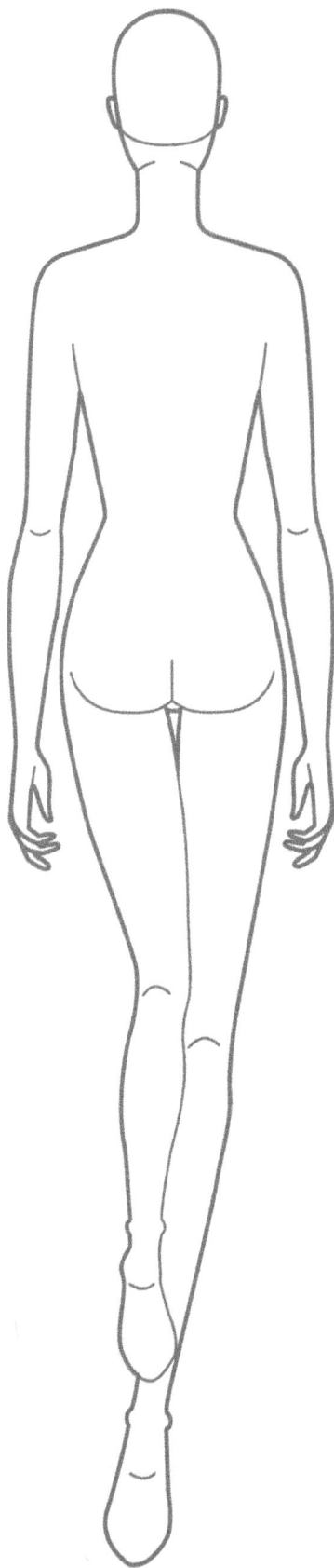

FASHION

FASHION

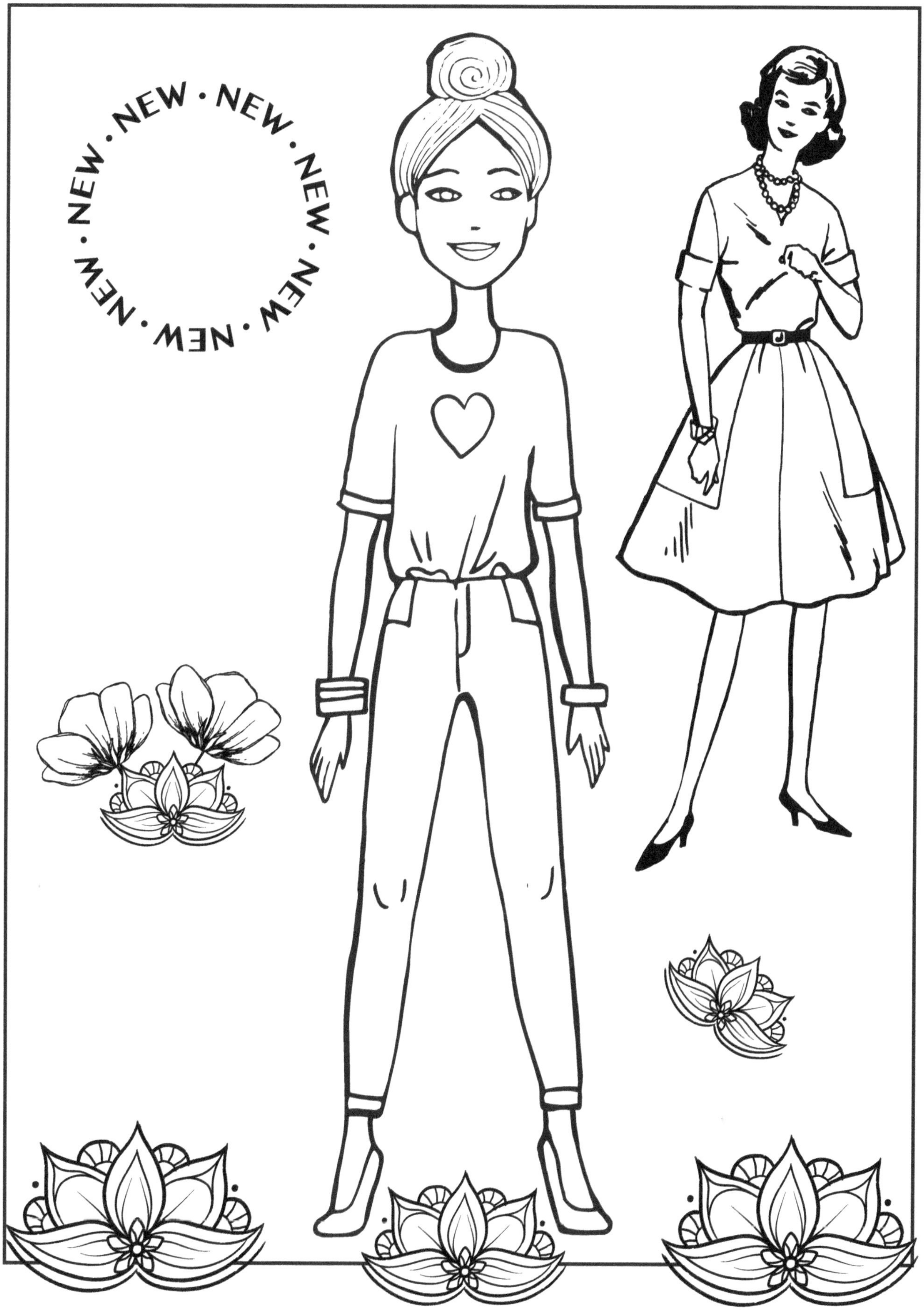
NEW · NEW · NEW · NEW · NEW · NEW · NEW · NEW · NEW ·

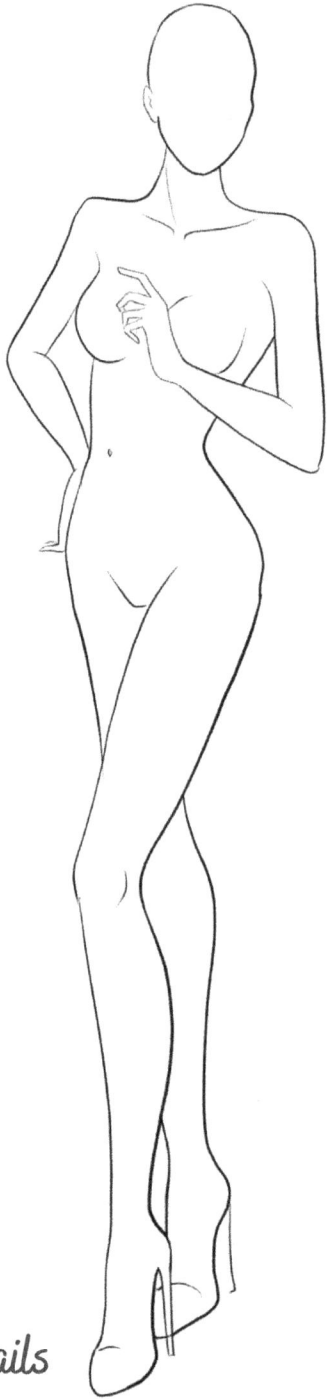

FASHION

Trends

_____
_____
_____

Inspiration

_____
_____
_____

Textiles

_____
_____
_____

Notes

_____
_____

Swatches

Details

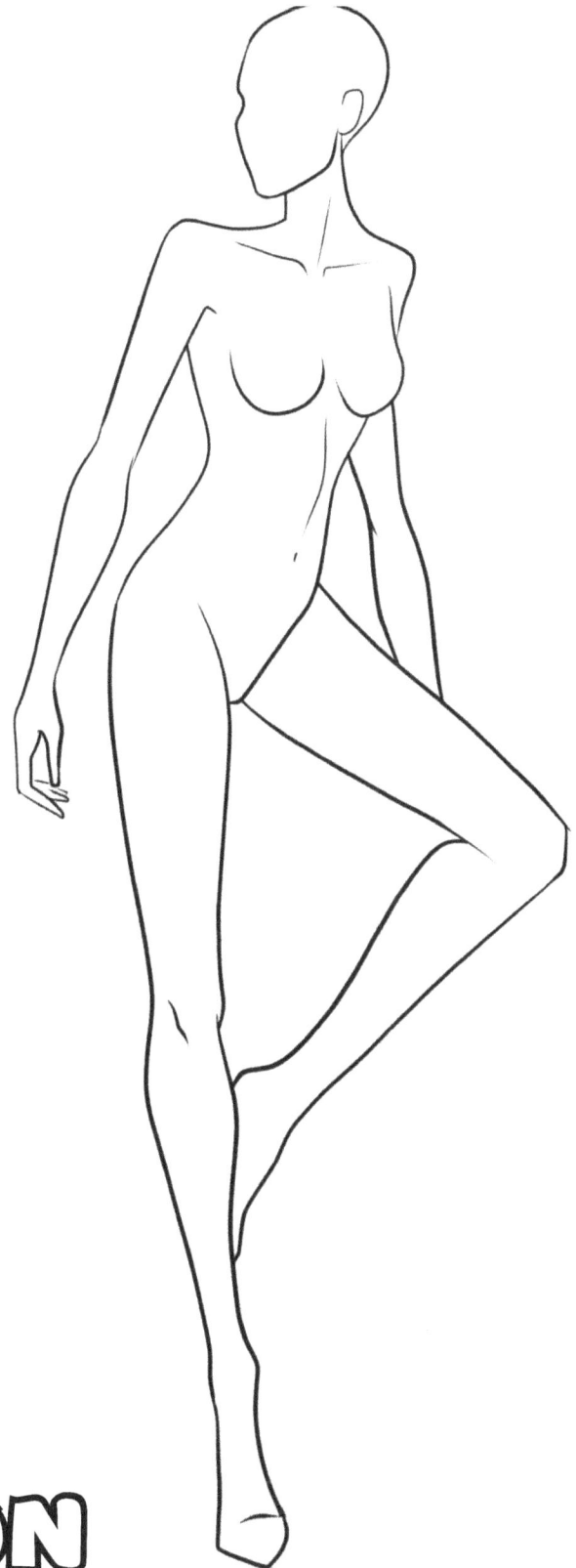

FASHION

FASHION

FASHION

STYLE · STYLE · STYLE · STYLE · STYLE · STYLE · STYLE · STYLE · STYLE · STYLE

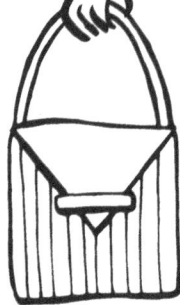

FASHION

FASHION

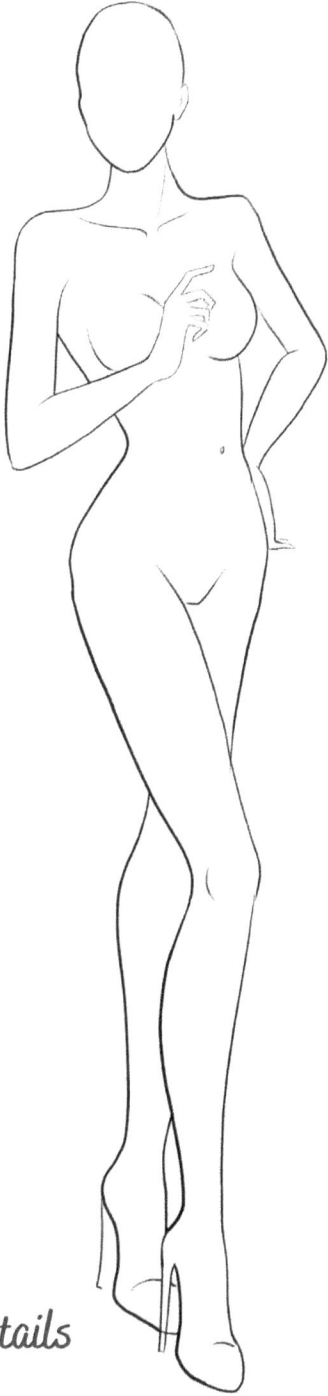

Trends

_____

_____

_____

Inspiration

_____

_____

_____

Textiles

_____

_____

_____

Notes

_____

_____

_____

Swatches

Details

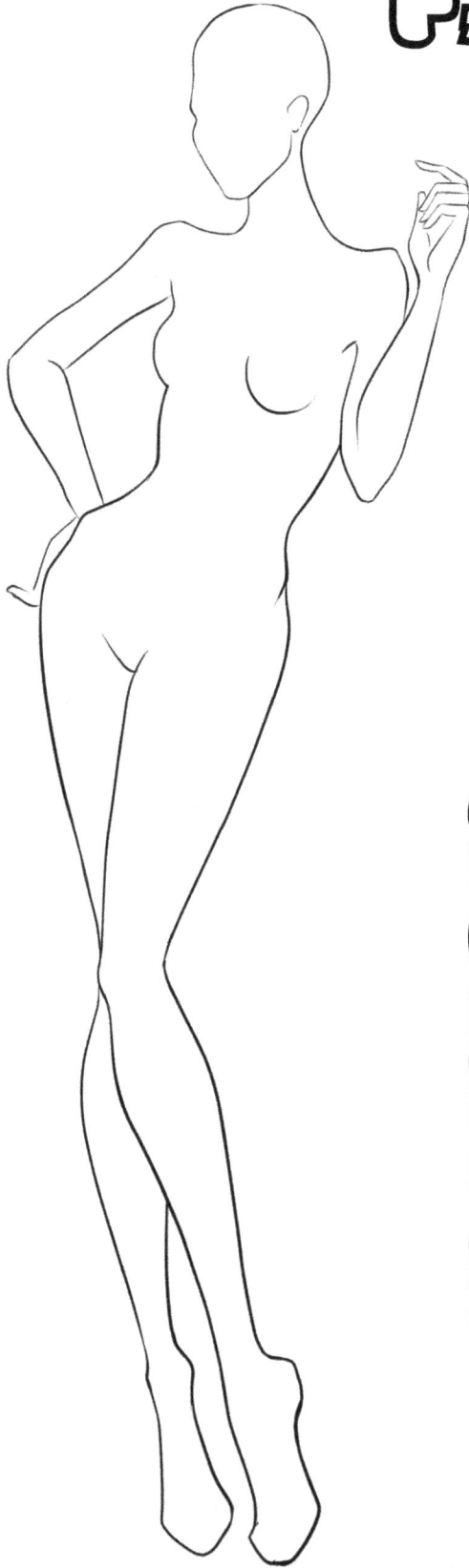

FASHION

FASHION

STYLE · STYLE · STYLE · STYLE · STYLE

FASHION

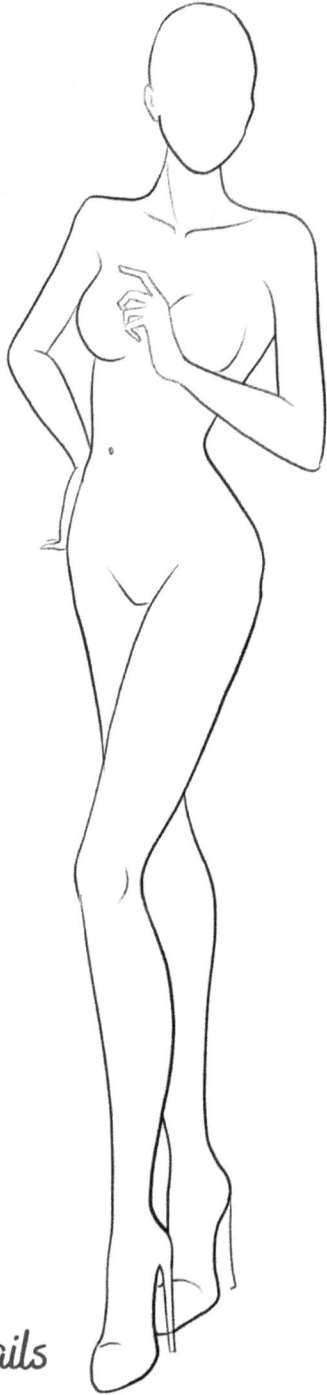

Trends

_____
_____
_____

Inspiration

_____
_____
_____

Textiles

_____
_____
_____

Notes

_____
_____

Swatches

Details

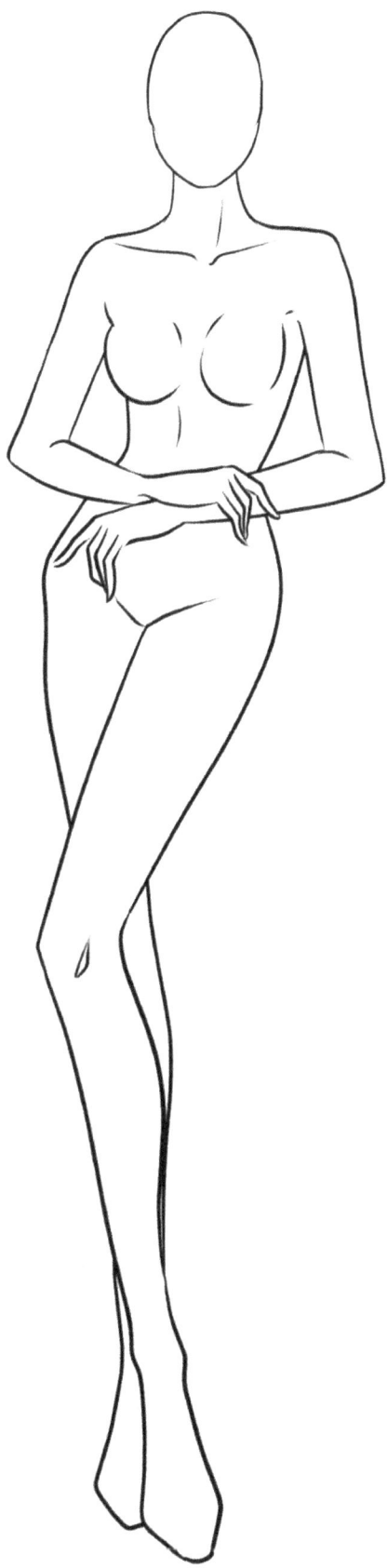

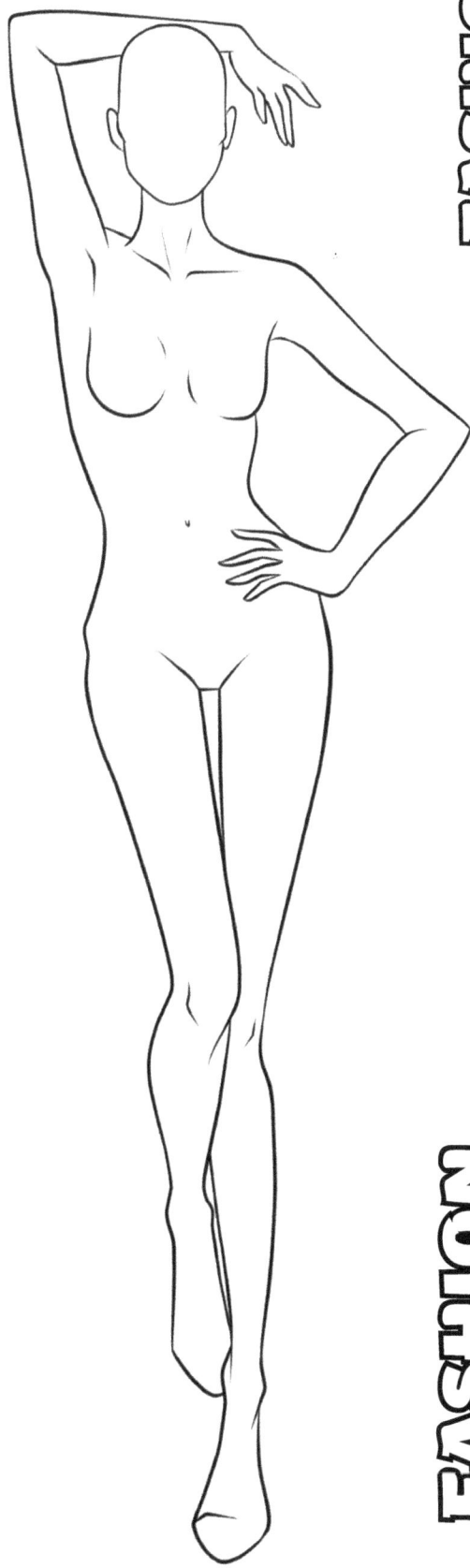

FASHION · FASHION · FASHION

FASHION

Trends
_____
_____
_____

Inspiration
_____
_____
_____

Textiles
_____
_____
_____

Notes
_____
_____
_____

Swatches

Details

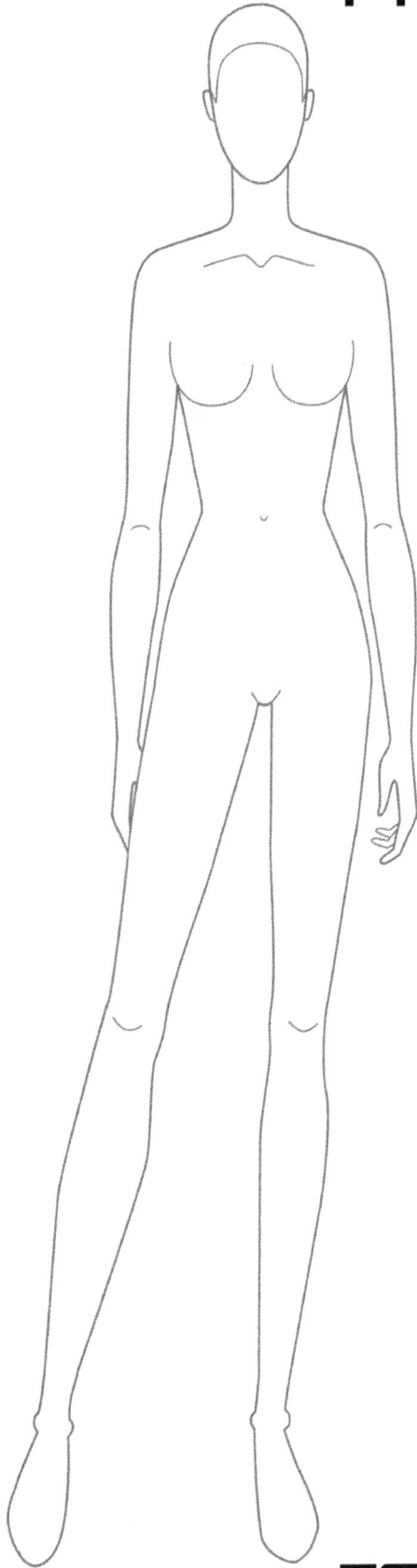

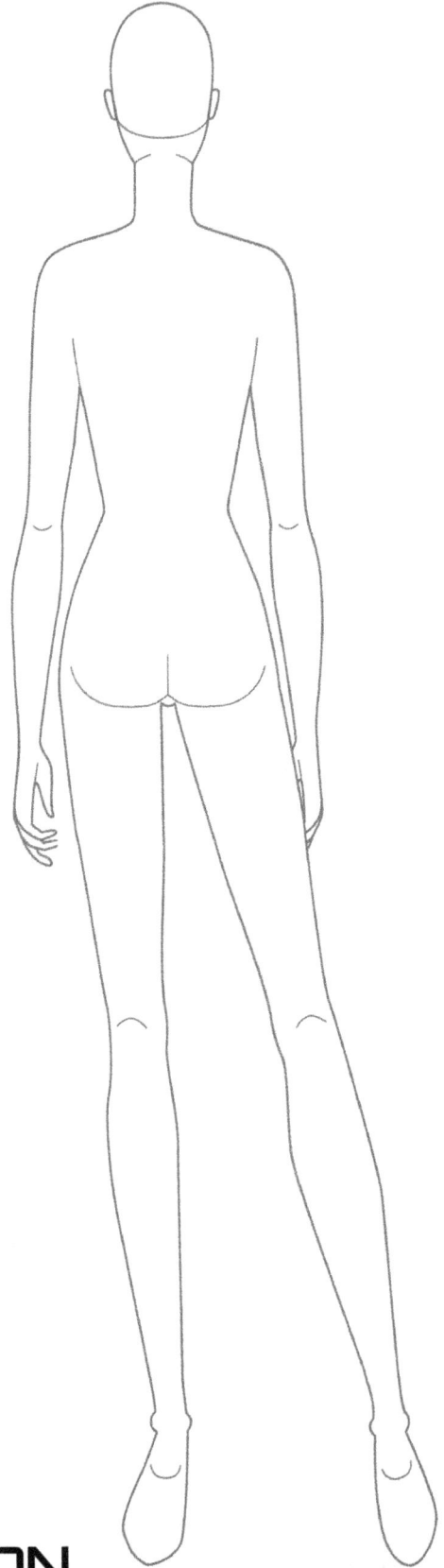

FASHION

FASHION

FASHION

FASHION

FASHION

Trends

_____

_____

_____

Inspiration

_____

_____

_____

_____

Textiles

_____

_____

_____

Notes

_____

_____

Swatches

Details

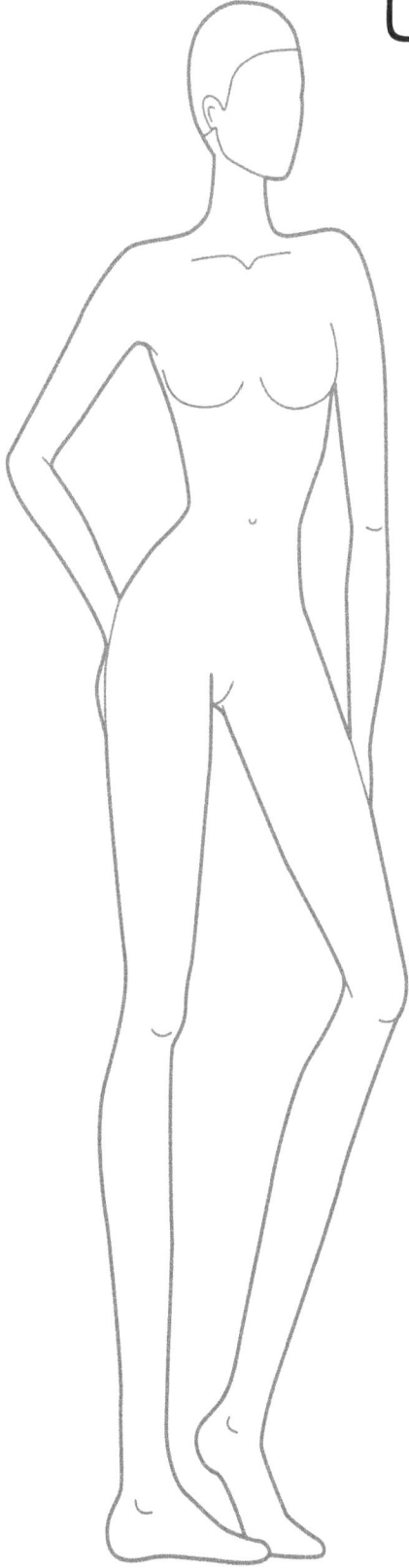

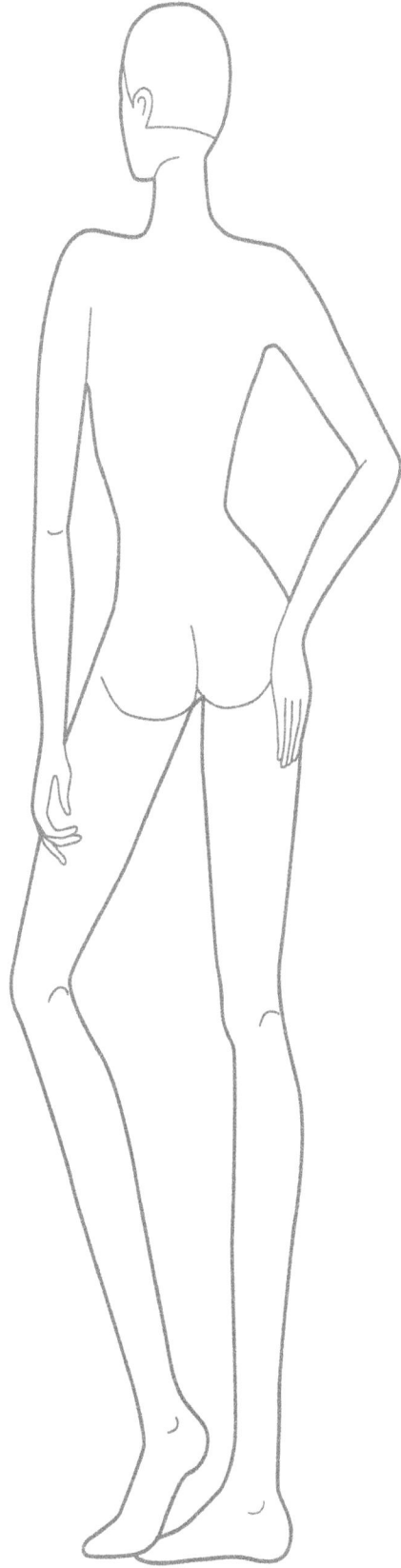

FASHION

FASHION

FASHION

FASHION

FASHION

FASHION · FASHION · FASHION · FASHION

FASHION

Trends
_____
_____
_____

Inspiration
_____
_____
_____

Textiles
_____
_____
_____

Notes
_____
_____

Swatches

Details

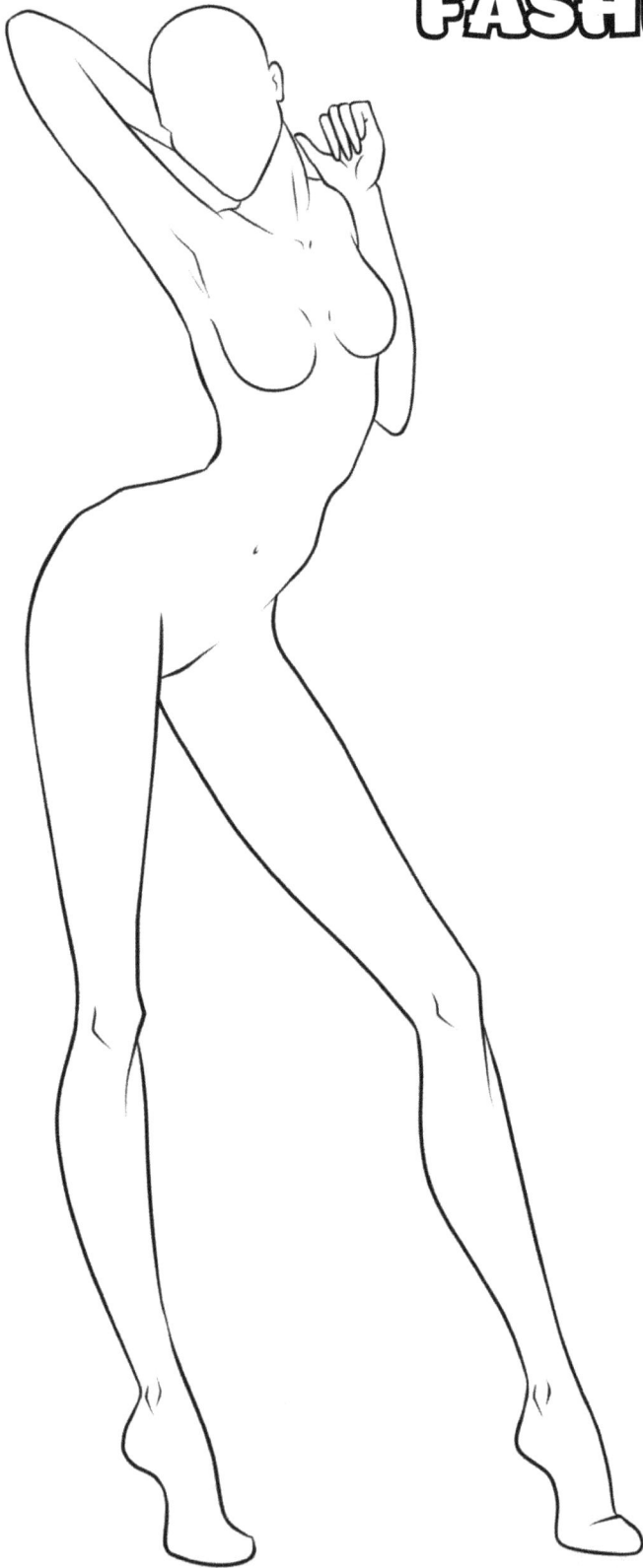

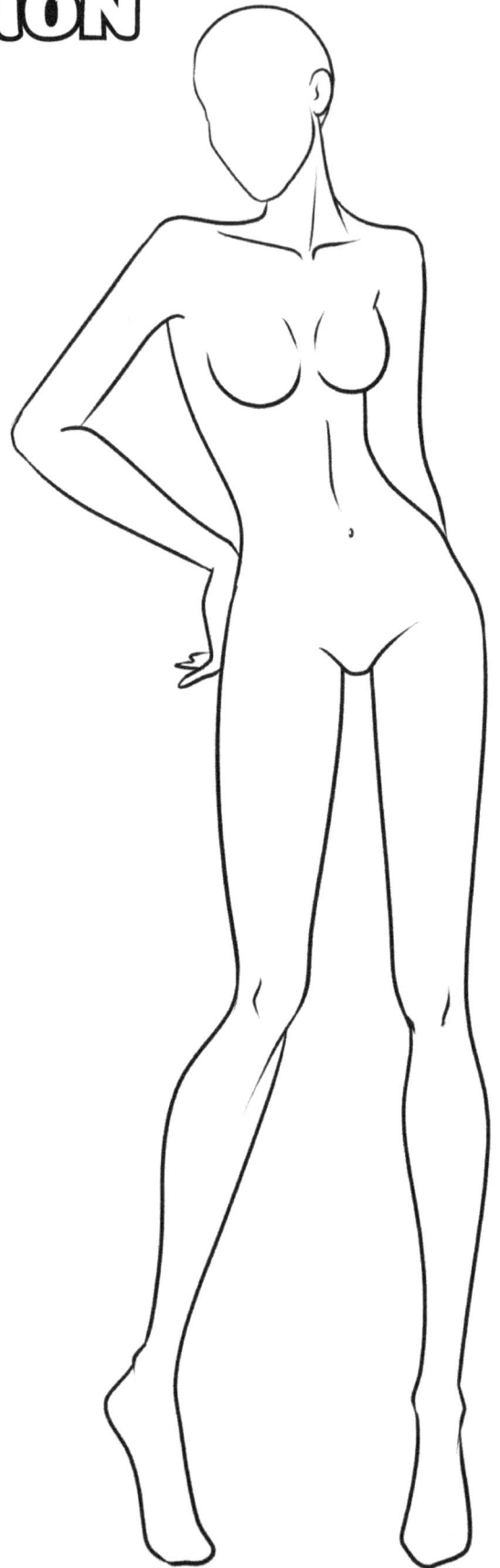

FASHION

FASHION

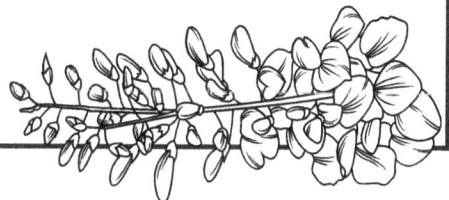

COLLECTION · COLLECTION ·

FASHION

Trends

_____

_____

_____

Inspiration

_____

_____

_____

Textiles

_____

_____

_____

Notes

_____

_____

Swatches

Details

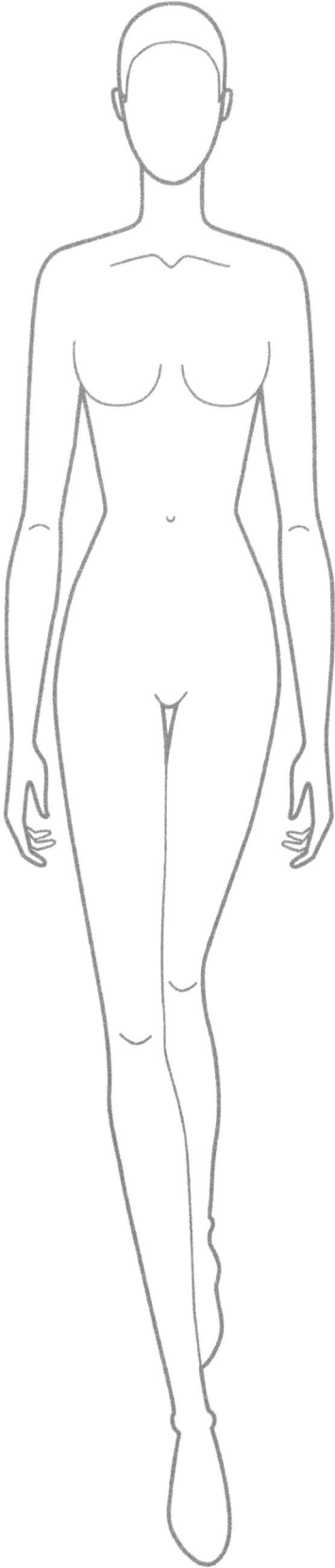

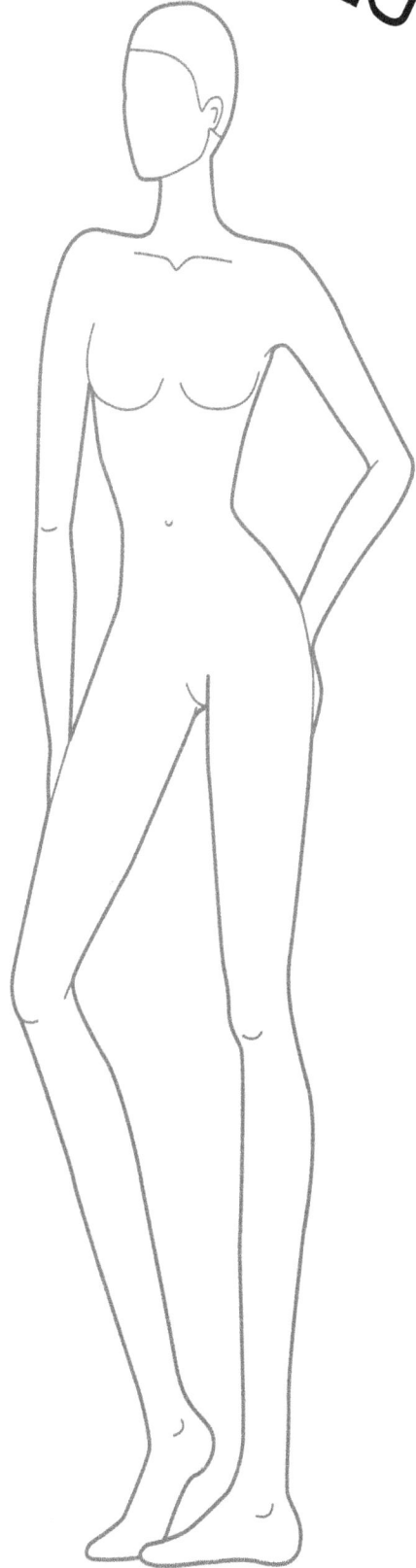

FASHION

FASHION

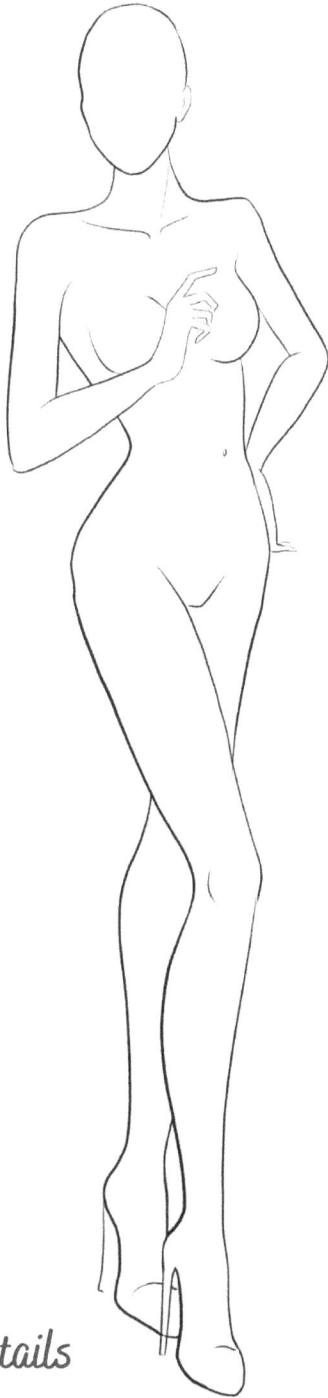

Trends

_____

_____

_____

Inspiration

_____

_____

_____

Textiles

_____

_____

_____

Notes

_____

_____

_____

FASHION

Swatches

Details

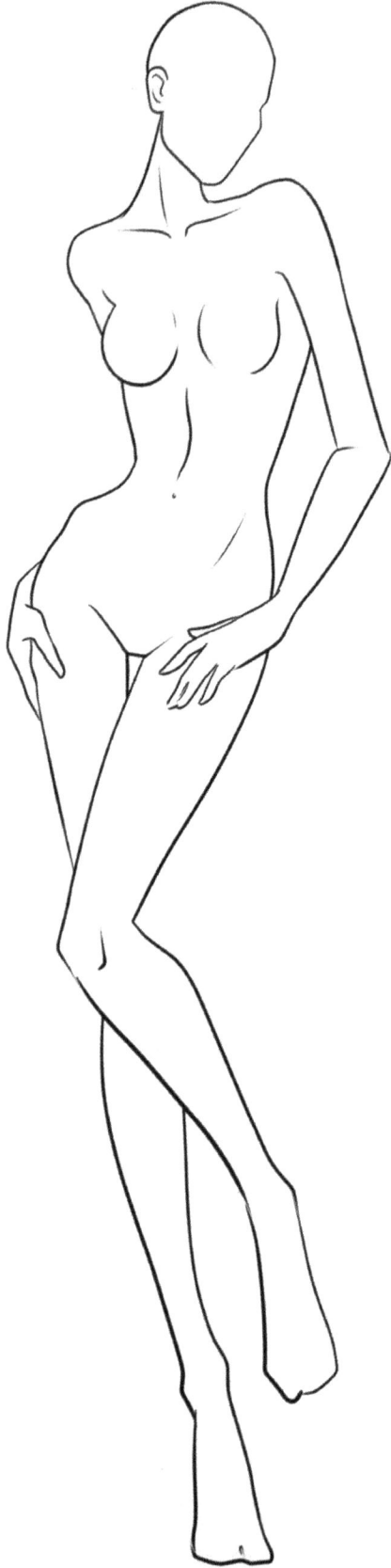

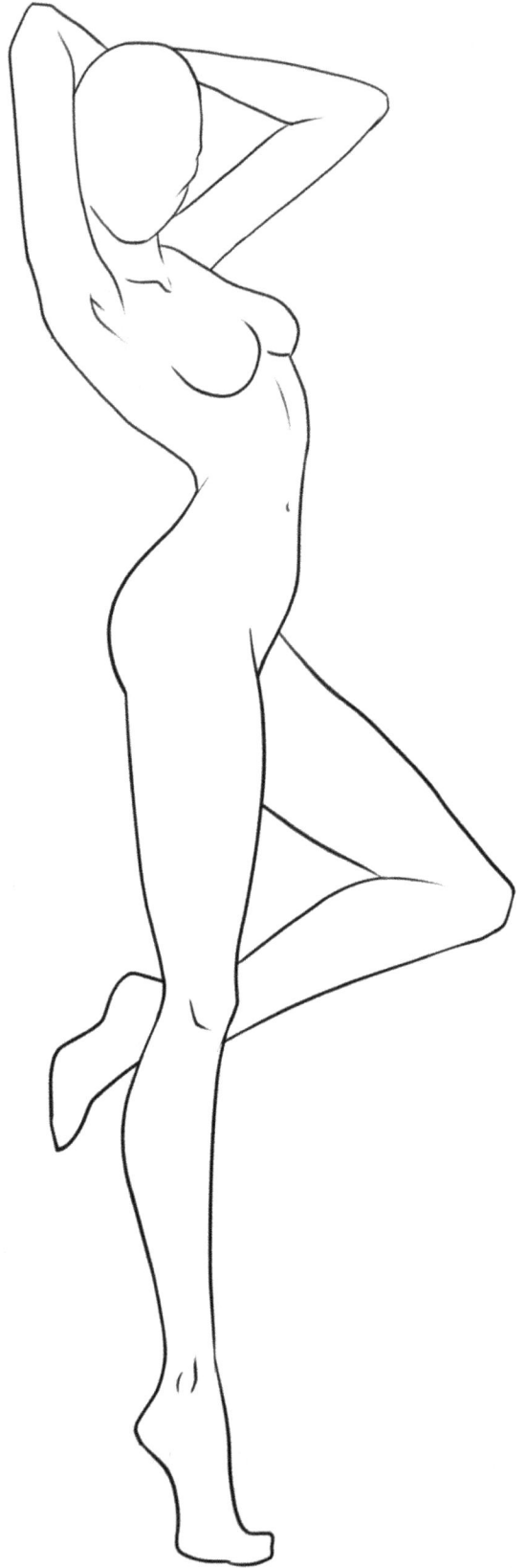

FASHION

FASHION

FASHION

FASHION FASHION FASHION

Trends

_____
_____
_____

Inspiration

_____
_____
_____
_____

Textiles

_____
_____
_____

Notes

_____
_____
_____

FASHION

Swatches

Details

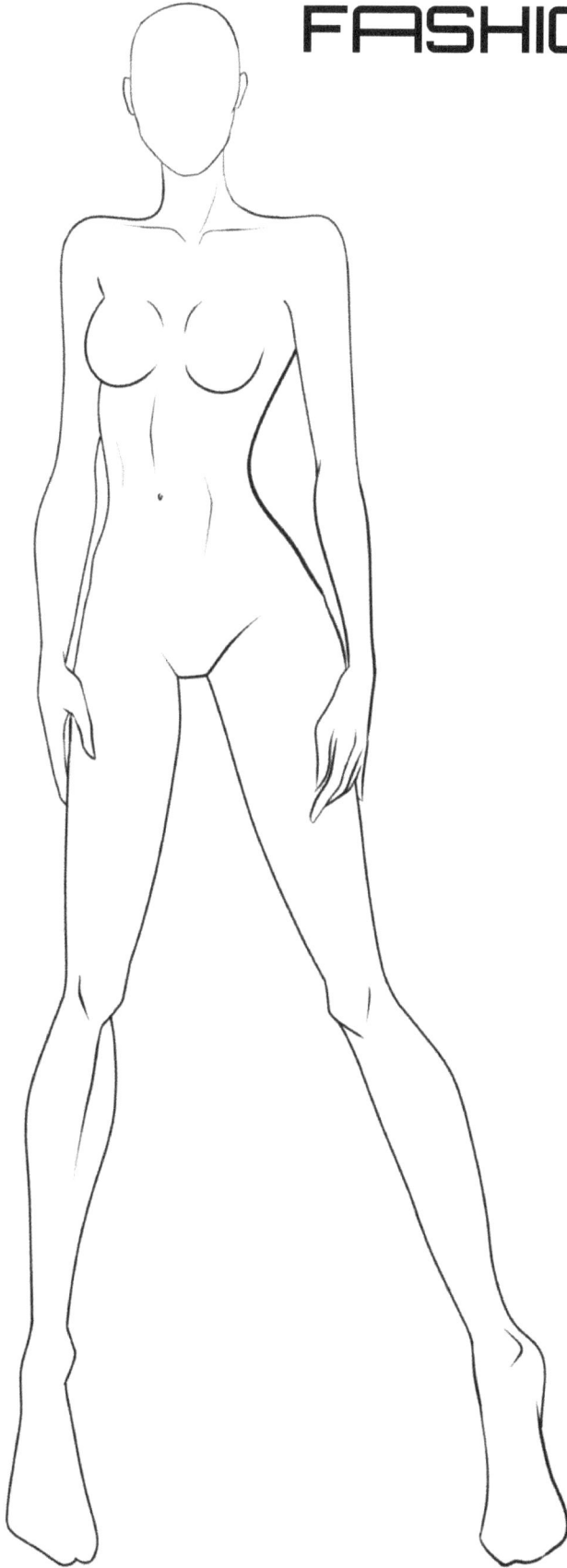

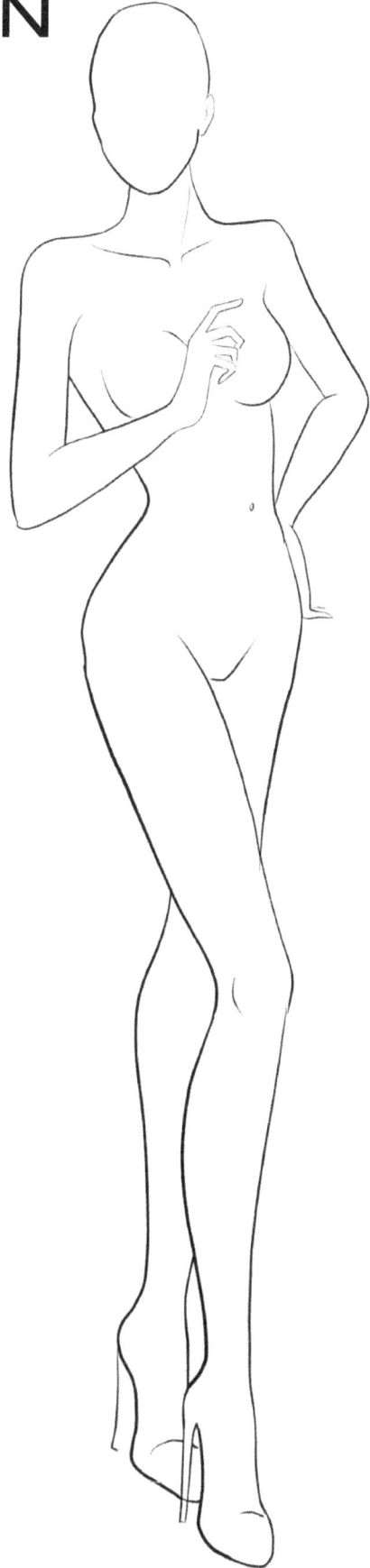

FASHION

FASHION

FASHION

STYLE · STYLE · STYLE · STYLE

FASHION

Trends
_____
_____
_____

Inspiration
_____
_____
_____
_____

Textiles
_____
_____
_____
_____

Notes
_____
_____
_____
_____

FASHION

Swatches

Details

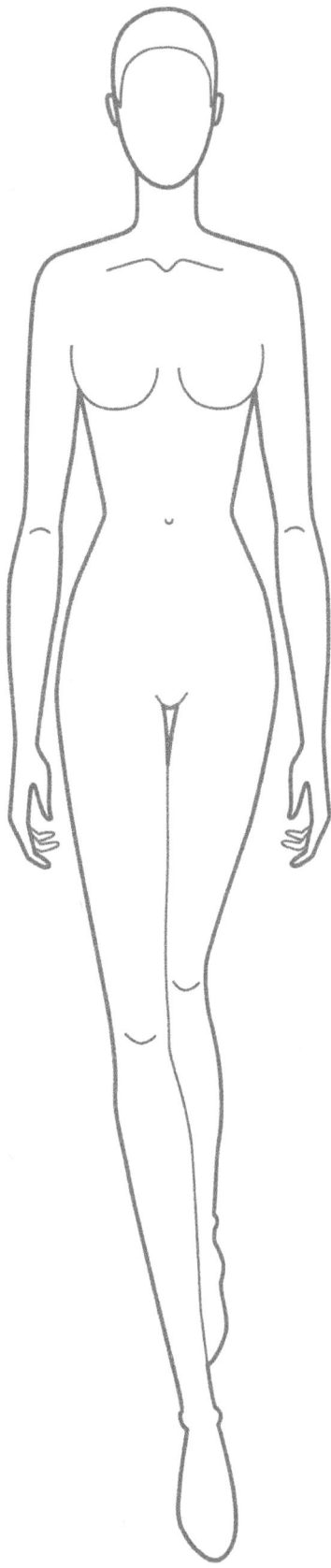

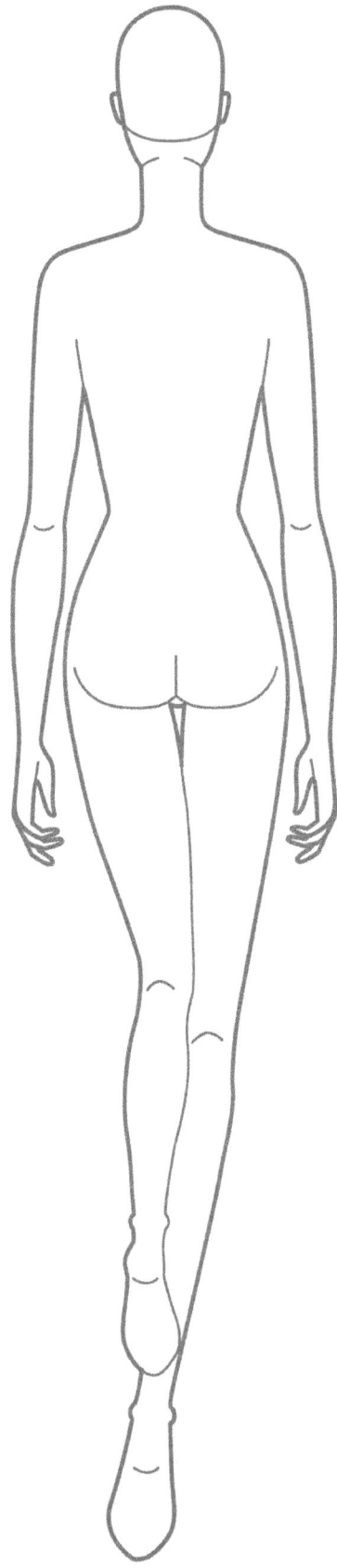

FASHION

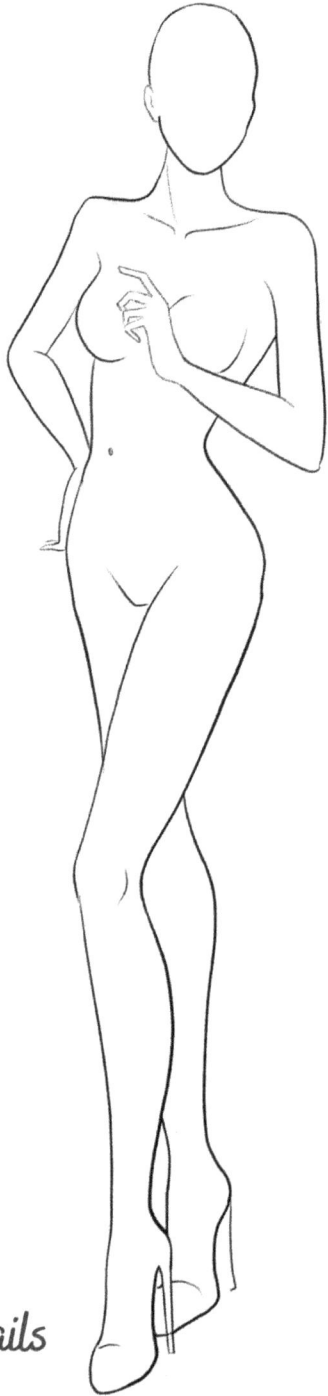

Trends

_____

_____

_____

Inspiration

_____

_____

_____

_____

Textiles

_____

_____

_____

Notes

_____

_____

_____

FASHION

Swatches

Details

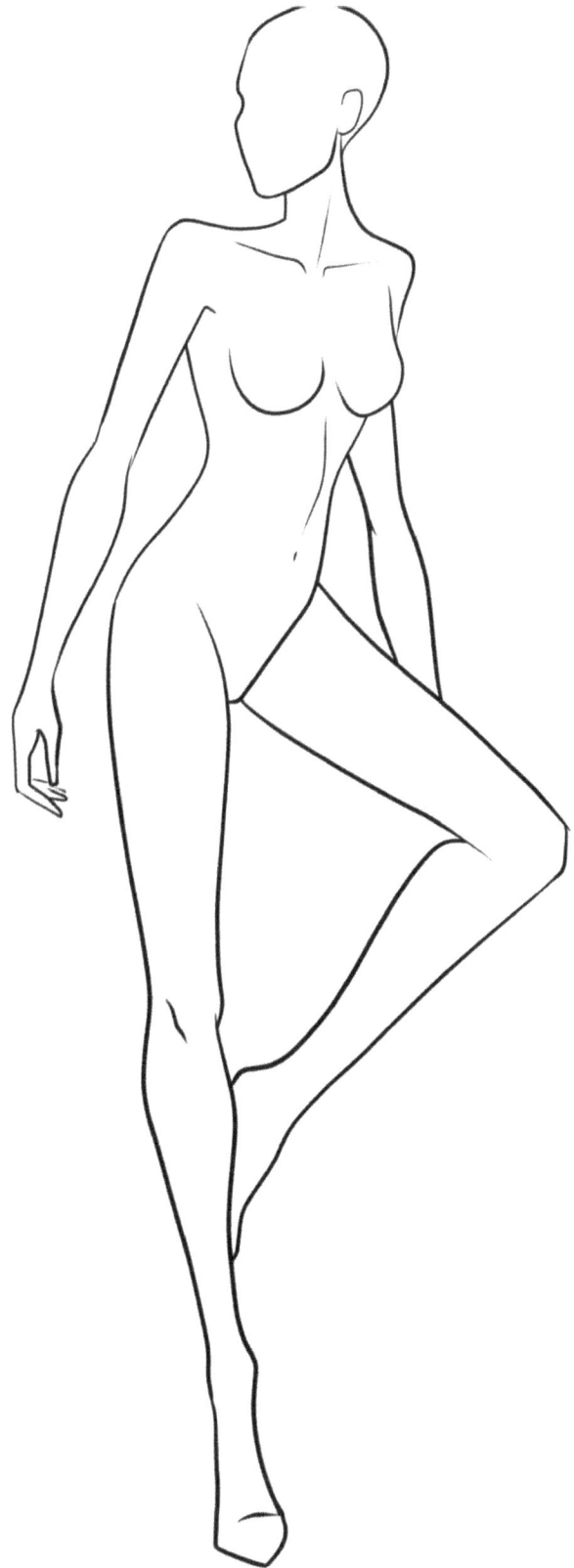

FASHION

FASHION

FASHION

Trends

_____

_____

_____

Inspiration

_____

_____

_____

Textiles

_____

_____

_____

Notes

_____

_____

_____

FASHION

Swatches

Details

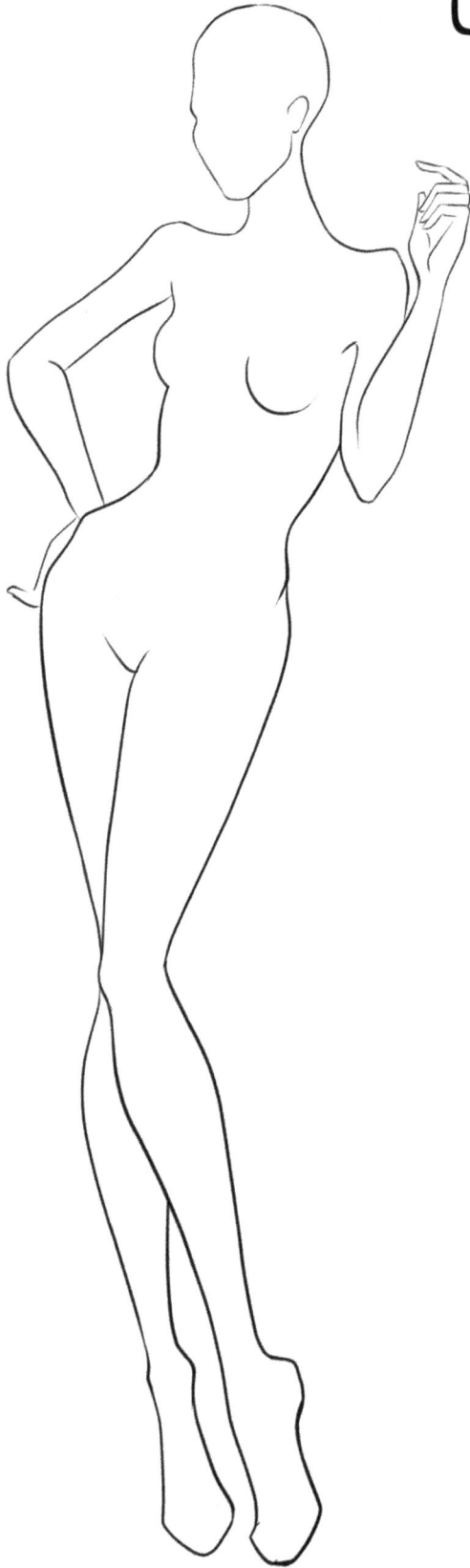

FASHION

FASHION

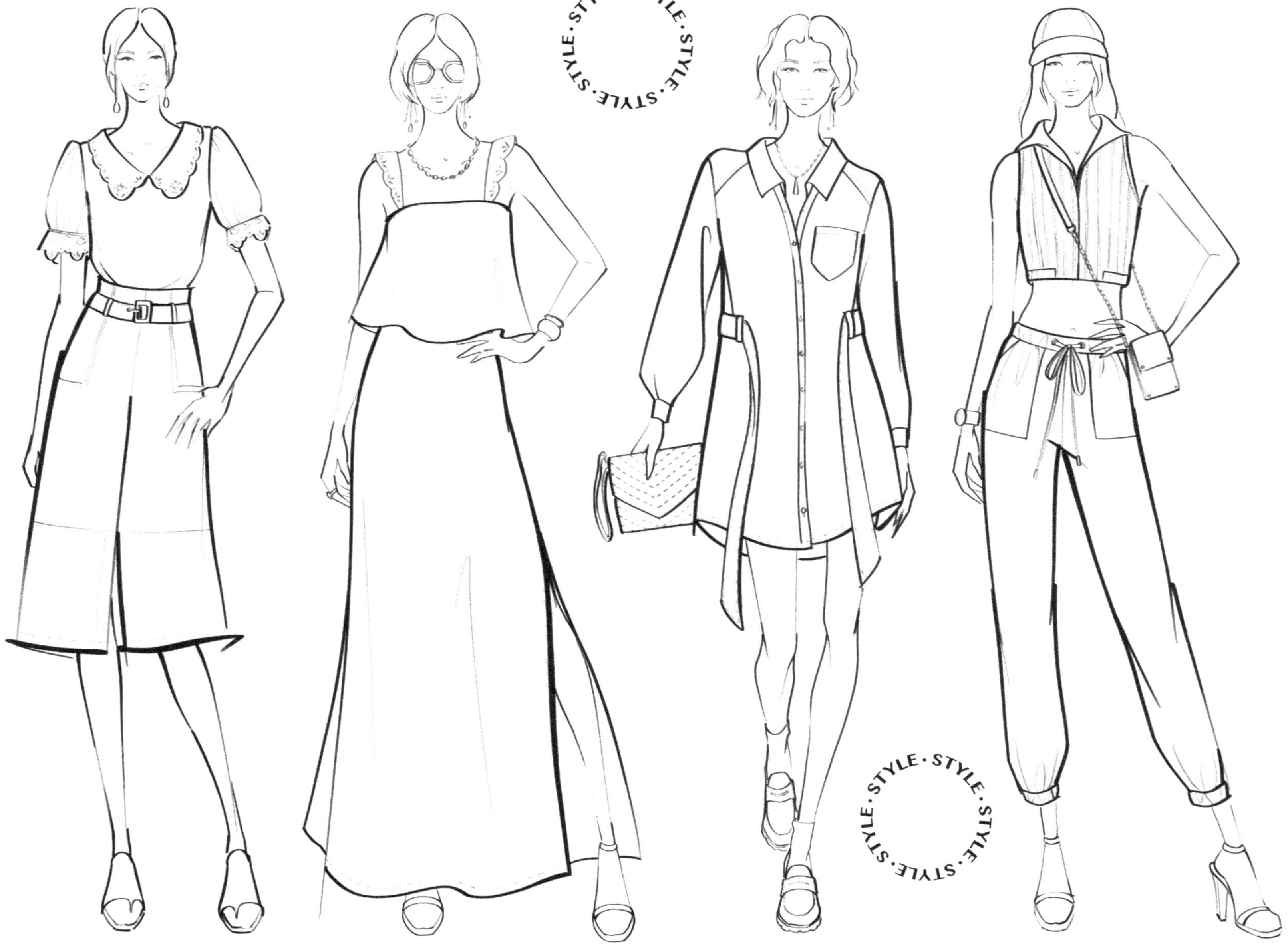
STYLE · STYLE · STYLE · STYLE ·
STYLE · STYLE · STYLE · STYLE ·

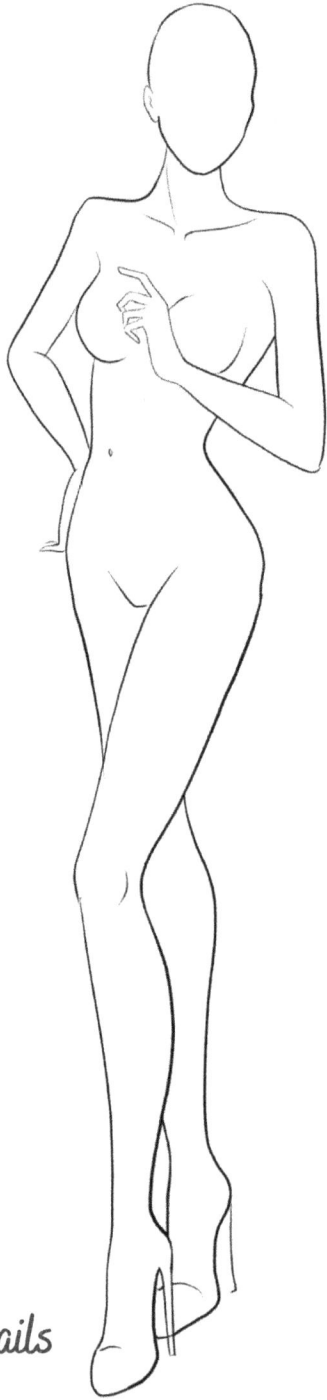

Trends
_____
_____
_____

Inspiration
_____
_____
_____
_____

Textiles
_____
_____
_____

Notes
_____
_____
_____

FASHION

Swatches

Details

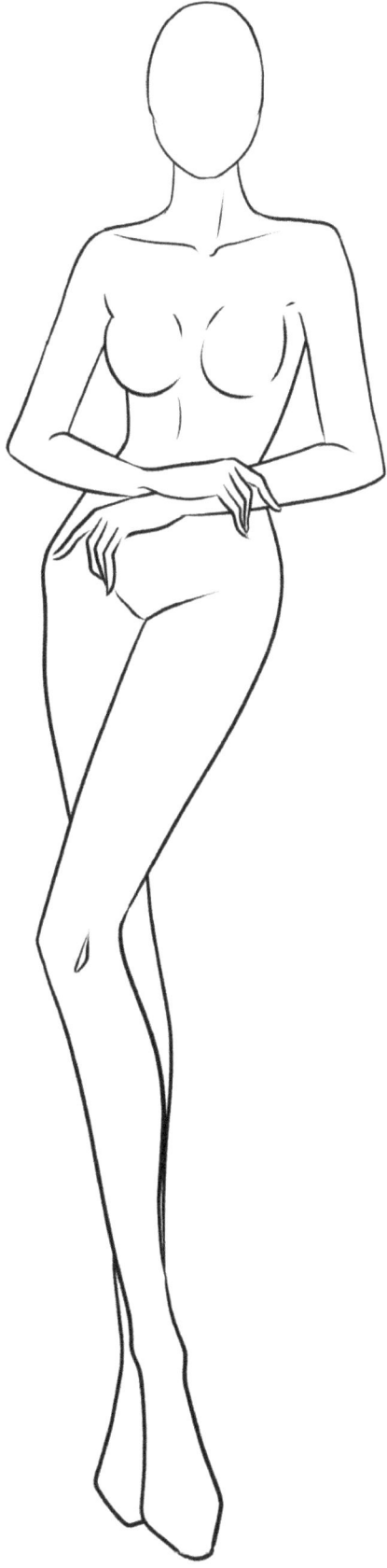

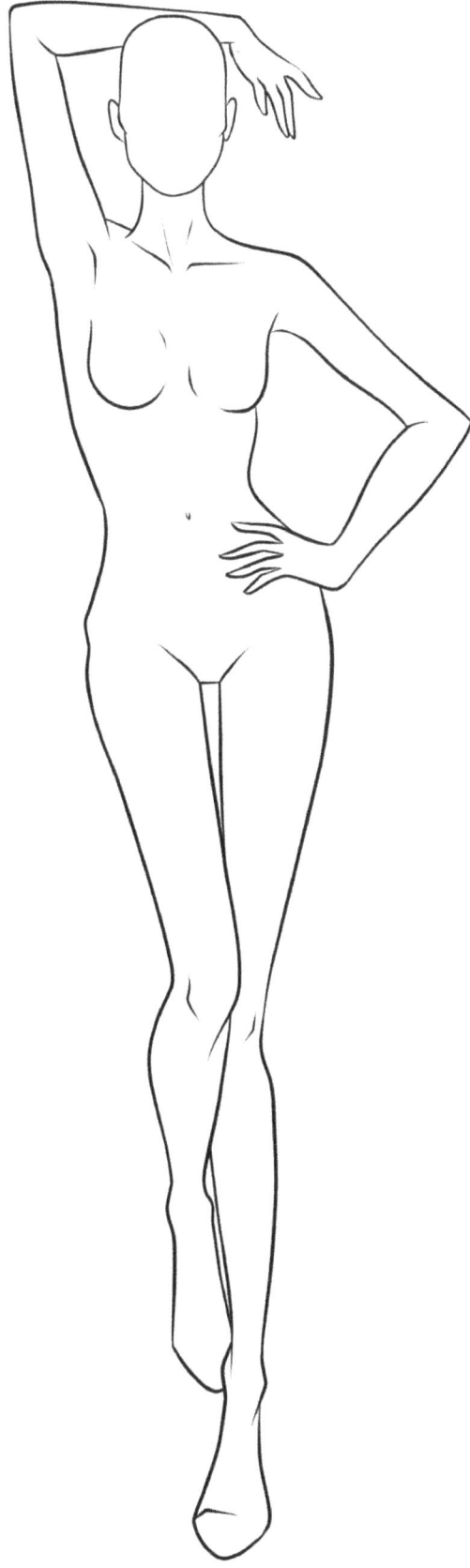

FASHION

FASHION

FASHION · FASHION ·
FASHION · FASHION ·
FASHION · FASHION ·
FASHION · FASHION ·
FASHION · FASHION ·

Trends

_____
_____
_____

Inspiration

_____
_____
_____

FASHION

Textiles

_____
_____
_____

Notes

_____
_____
_____

Swatches

Details

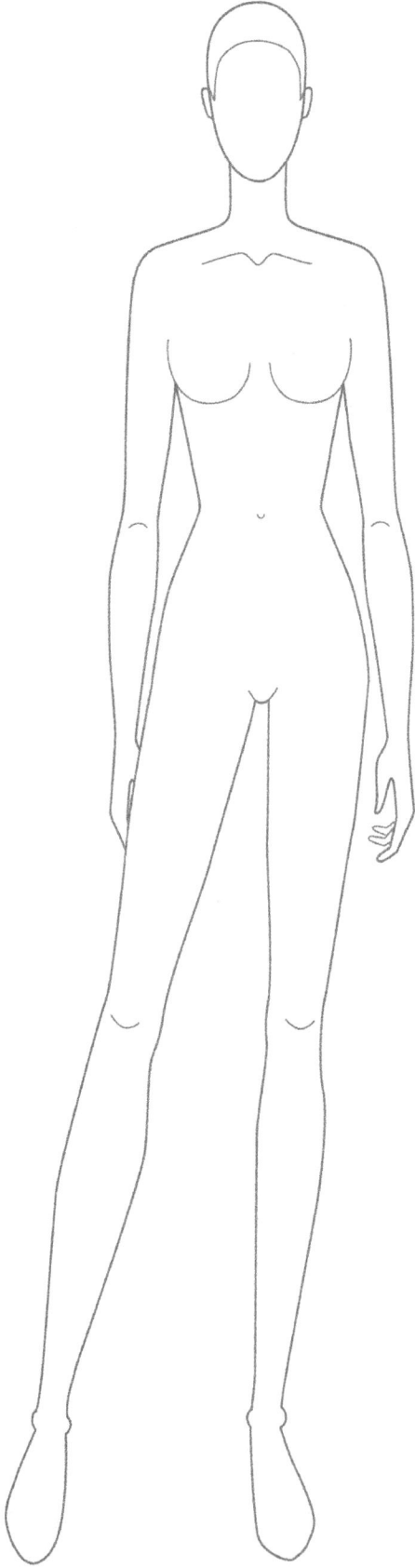

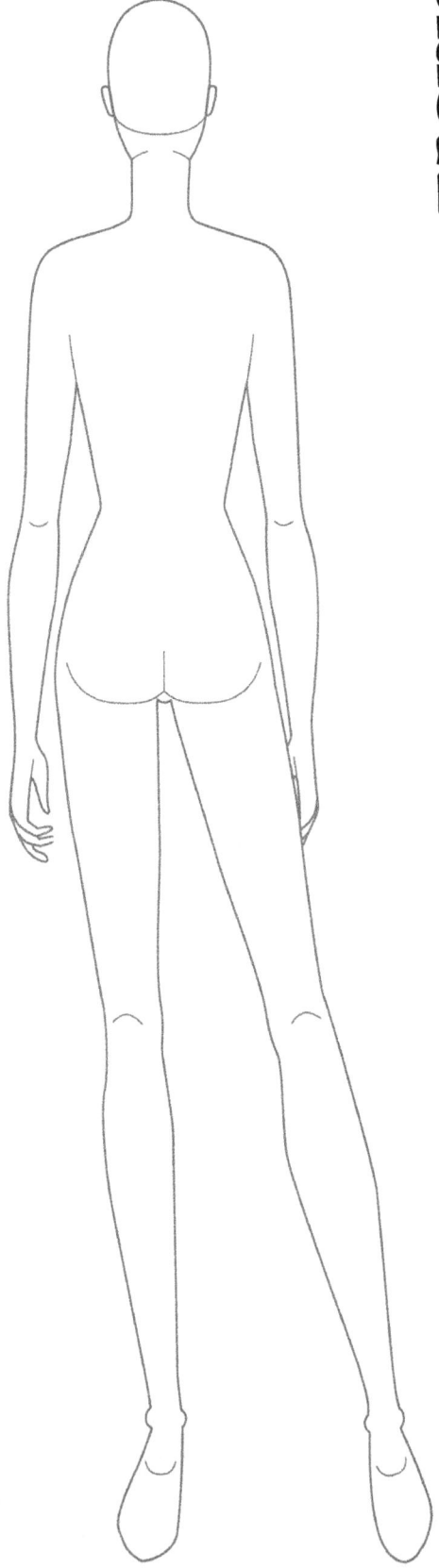

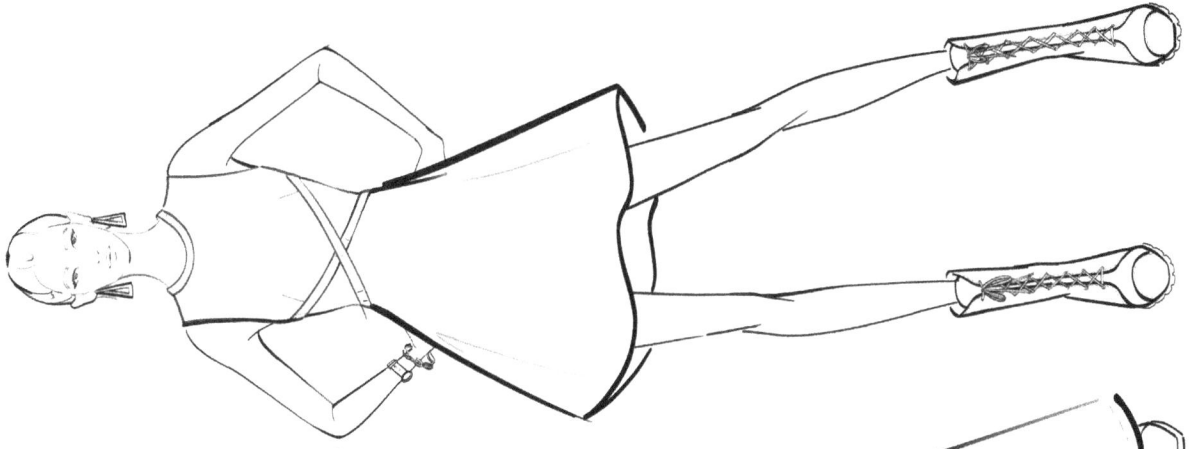

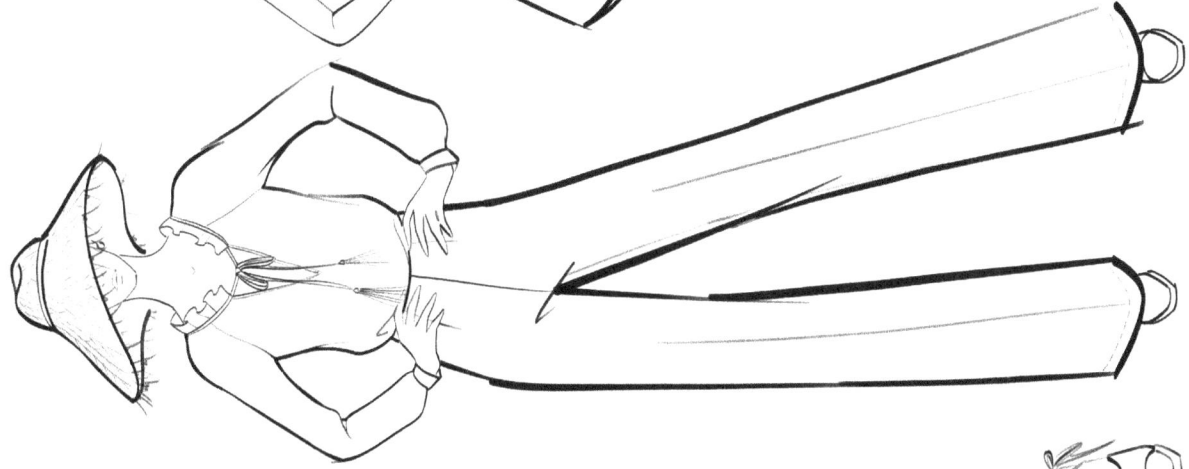

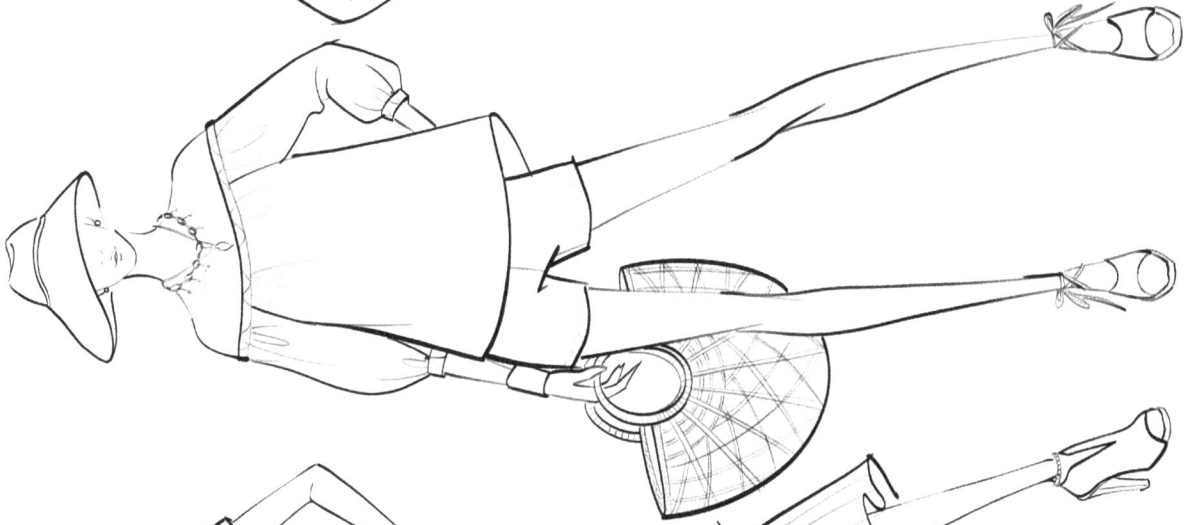

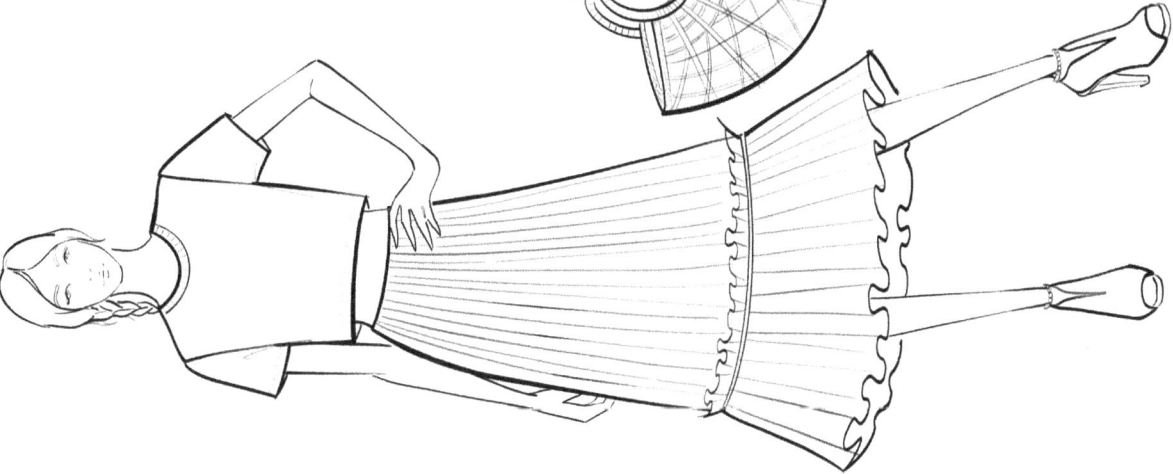

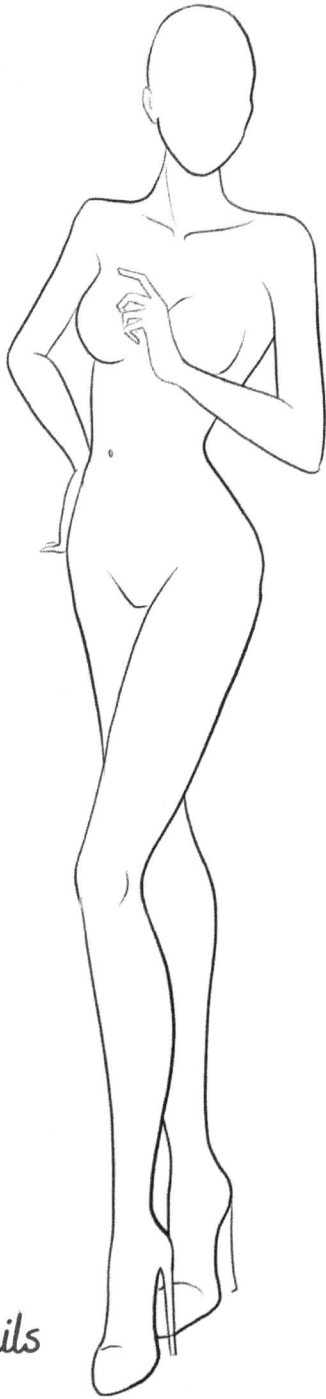

Trends

_____

_____

_____

Inspiration

_____

_____

_____

Textiles

_____

_____

_____

FASHION

Notes

_____

_____

_____

Swatches

Details

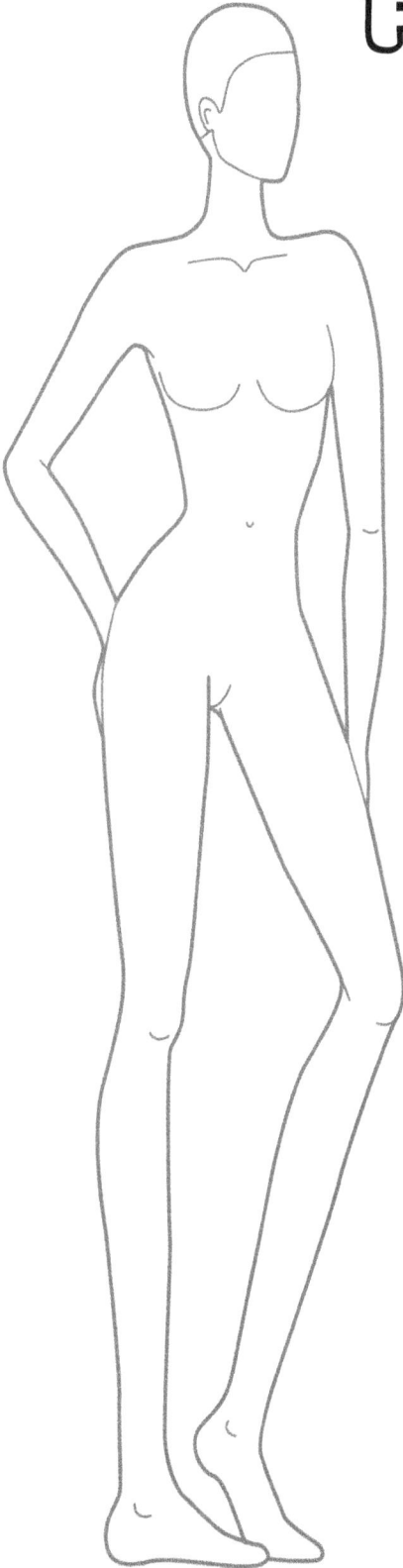

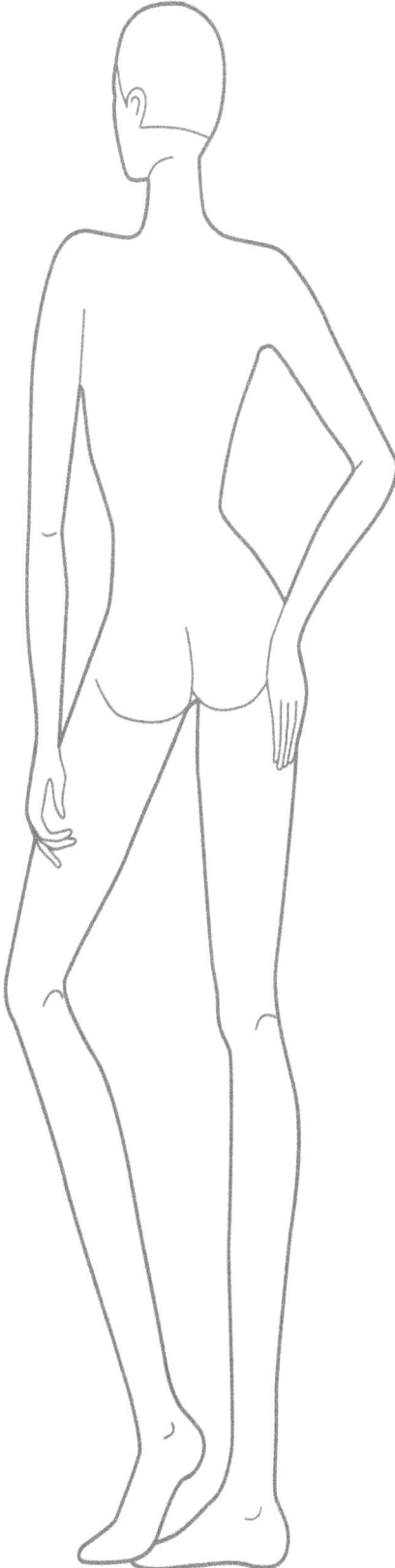

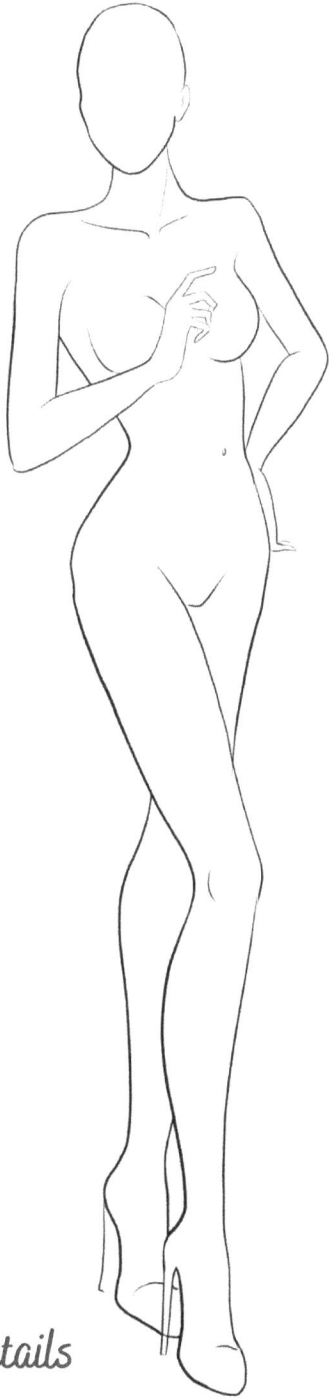

Trends

_____
_____
_____

Inspiration

_____
_____
_____

Textiles

_____
_____
_____

Notes

_____
_____
_____

FASHION

Details

Swatches

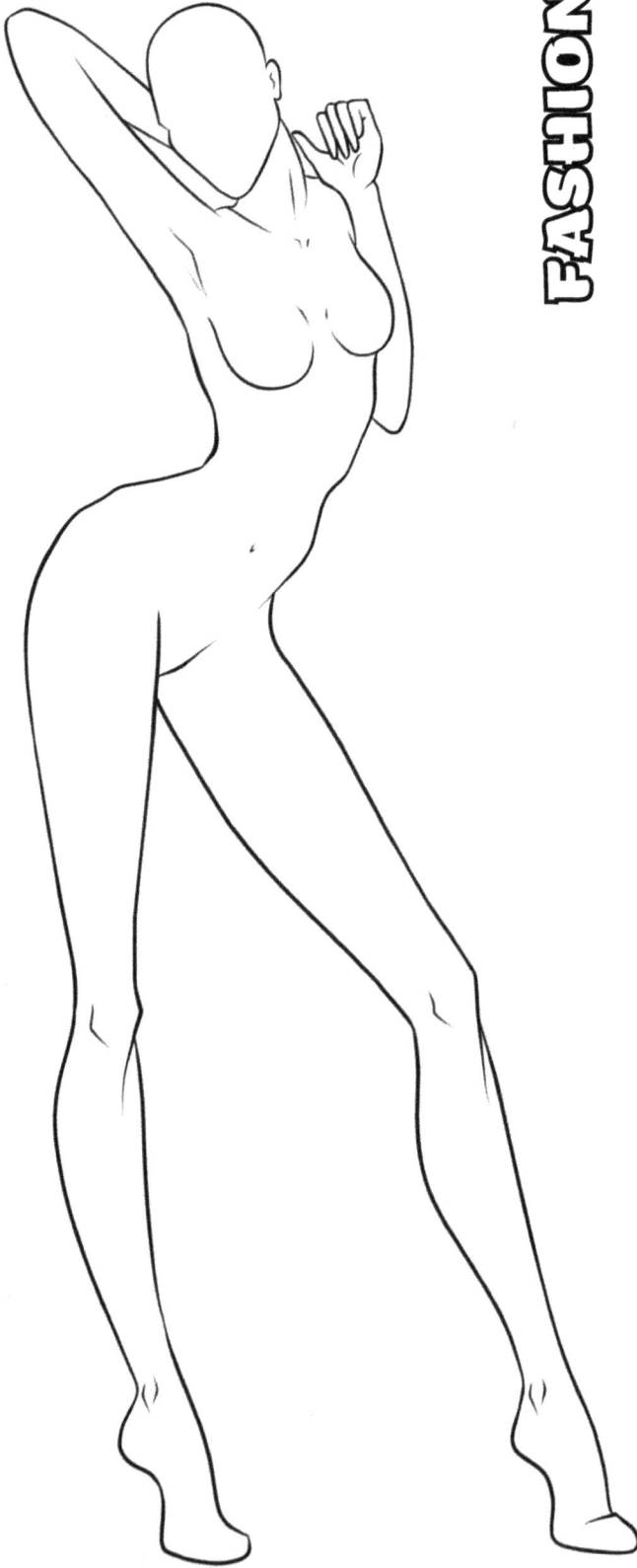

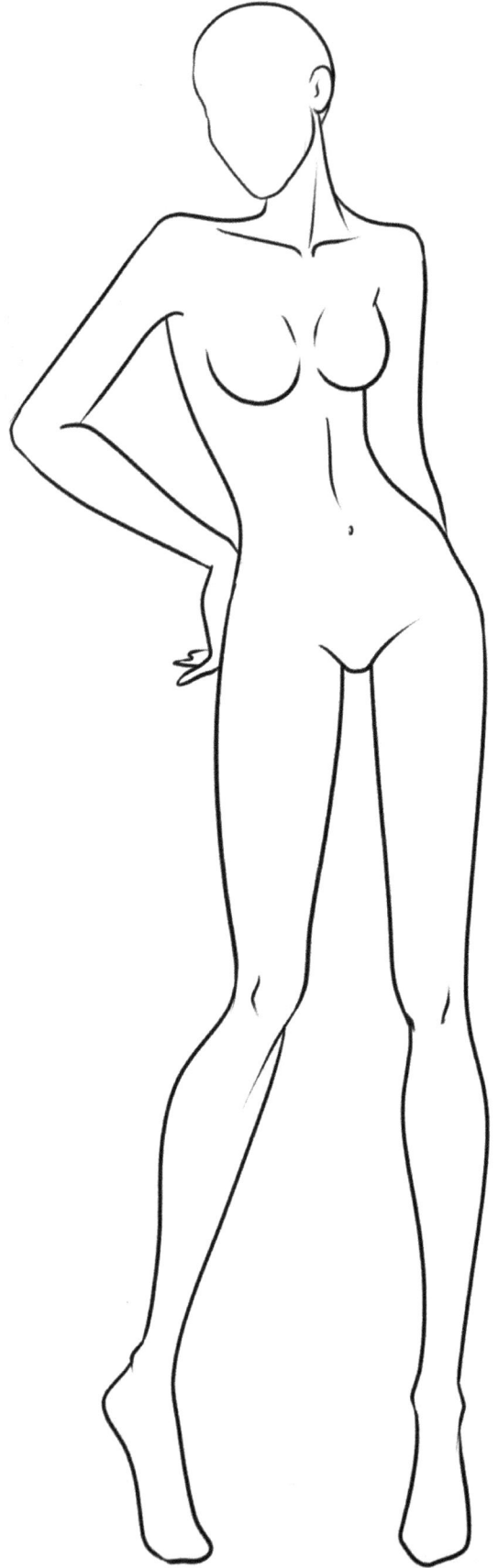

FASHION

FASHION

FASHION

FASHION

Trends

_____

_____

_____

Inspiration

_____

_____

_____

Textiles

_____

_____

_____

Notes

_____

_____

_____

FASHION

Details

Swatches

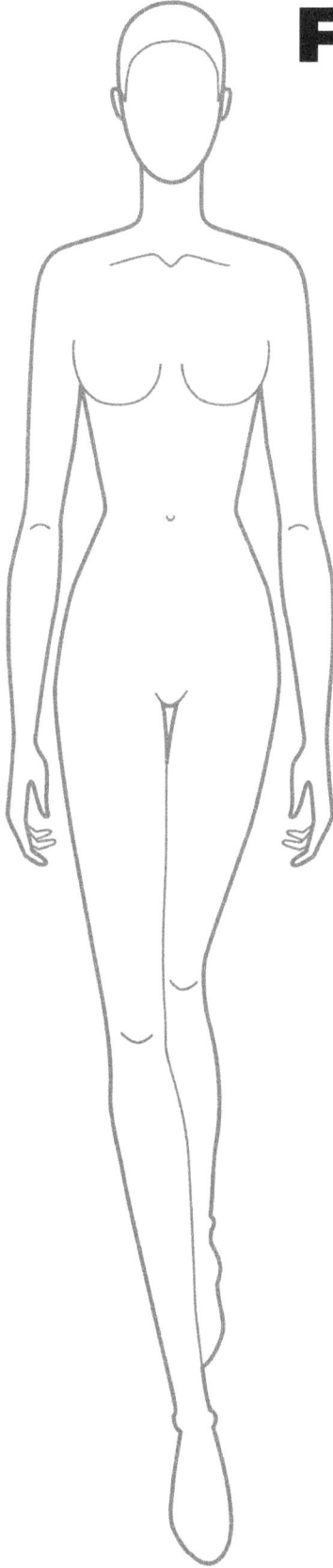

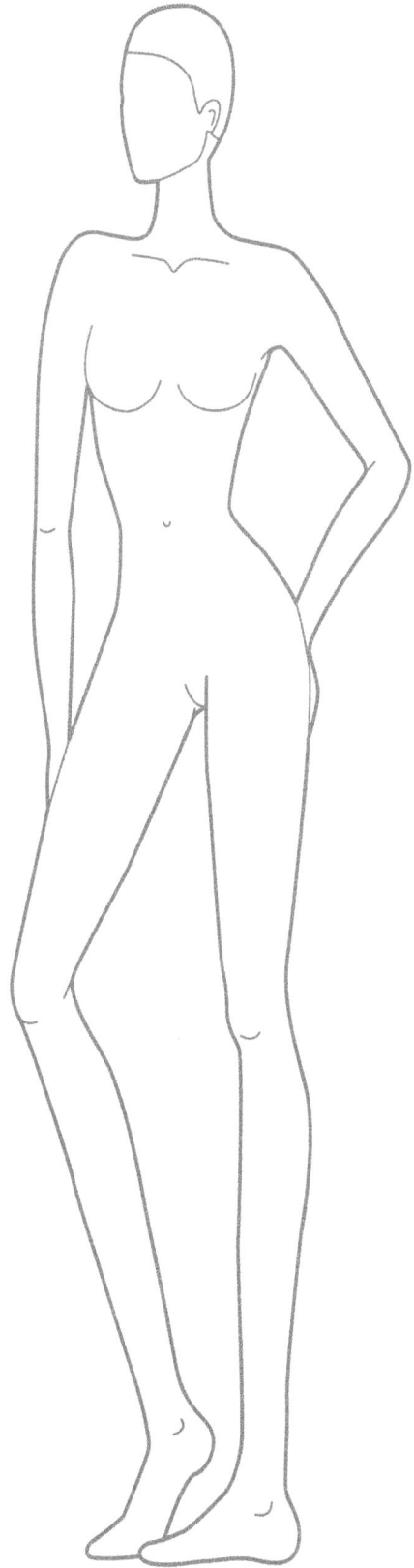

FASHION

FASHION

FASHION

Trends

_____

_____

_____

Inspiration

_____

_____

_____

Textiles

_____

_____

_____

Notes

_____

_____

Details

Swatches

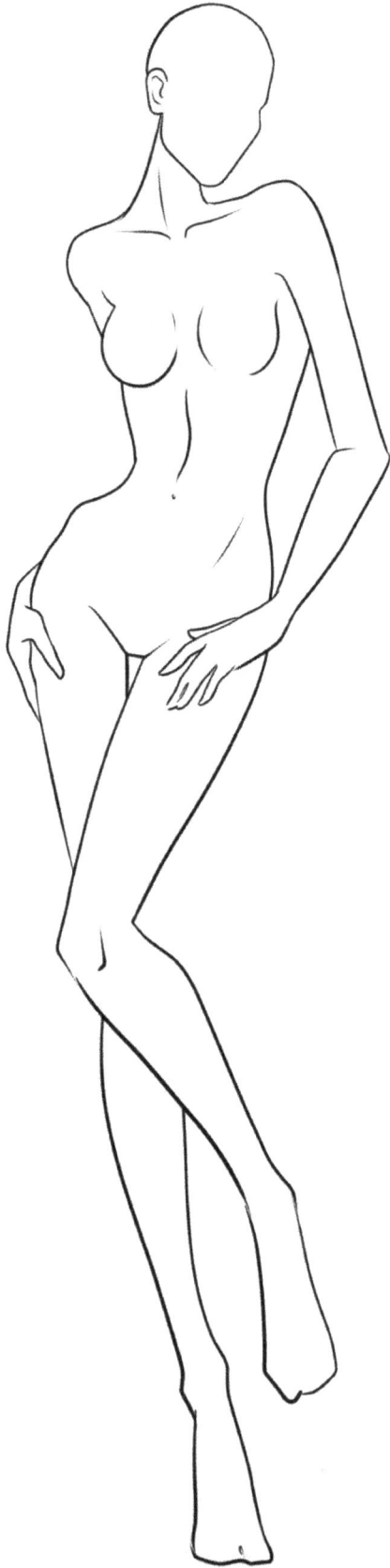

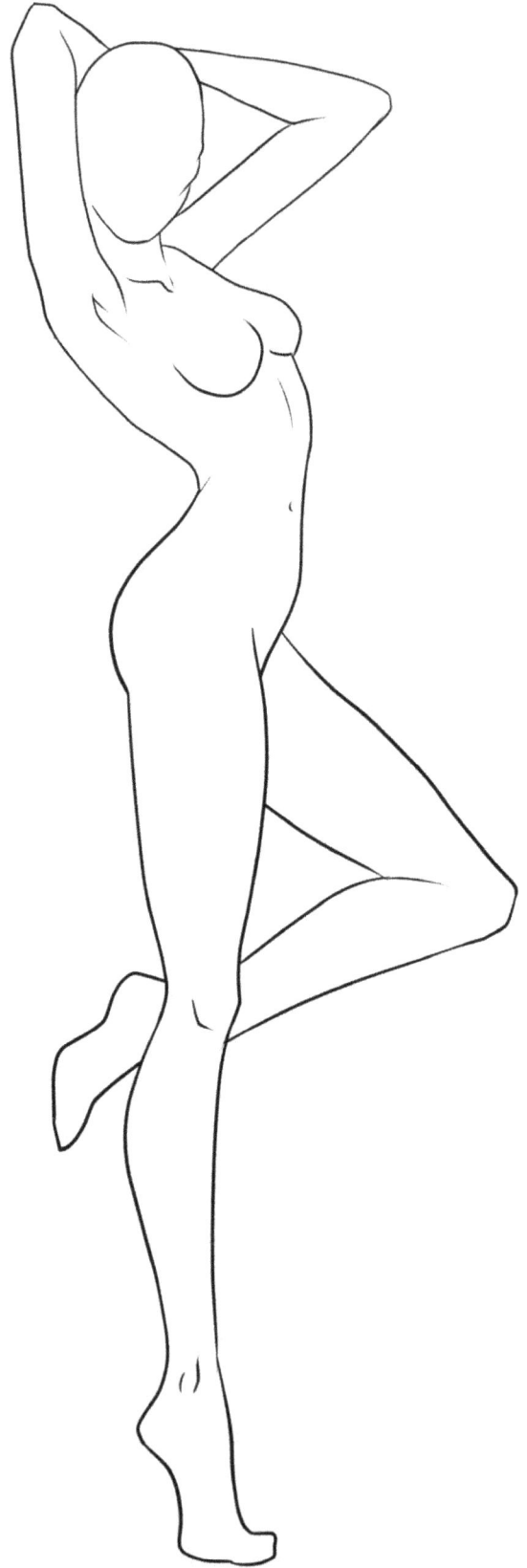

FASHION

FASHION

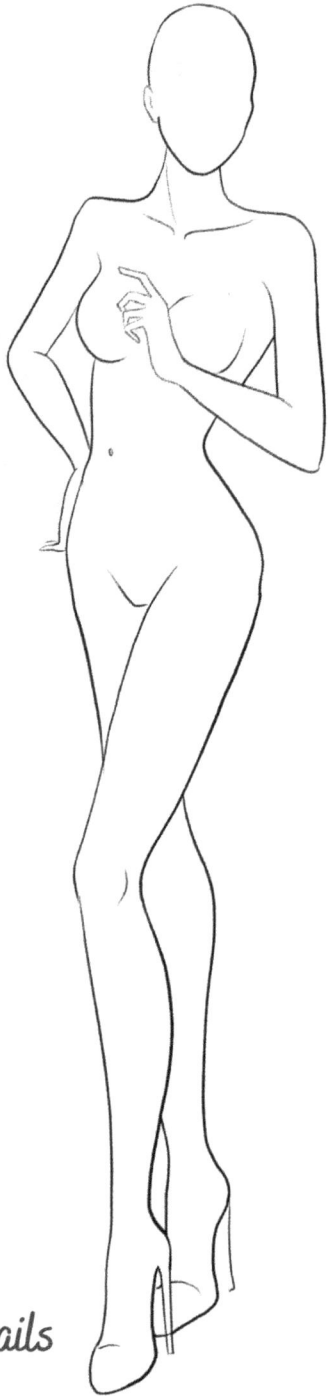

FASHION

Trends

_____

_____

_____

Inspiration

_____

_____

_____

Textiles

_____

_____

_____

Notes

_____

_____

Details

Swatches

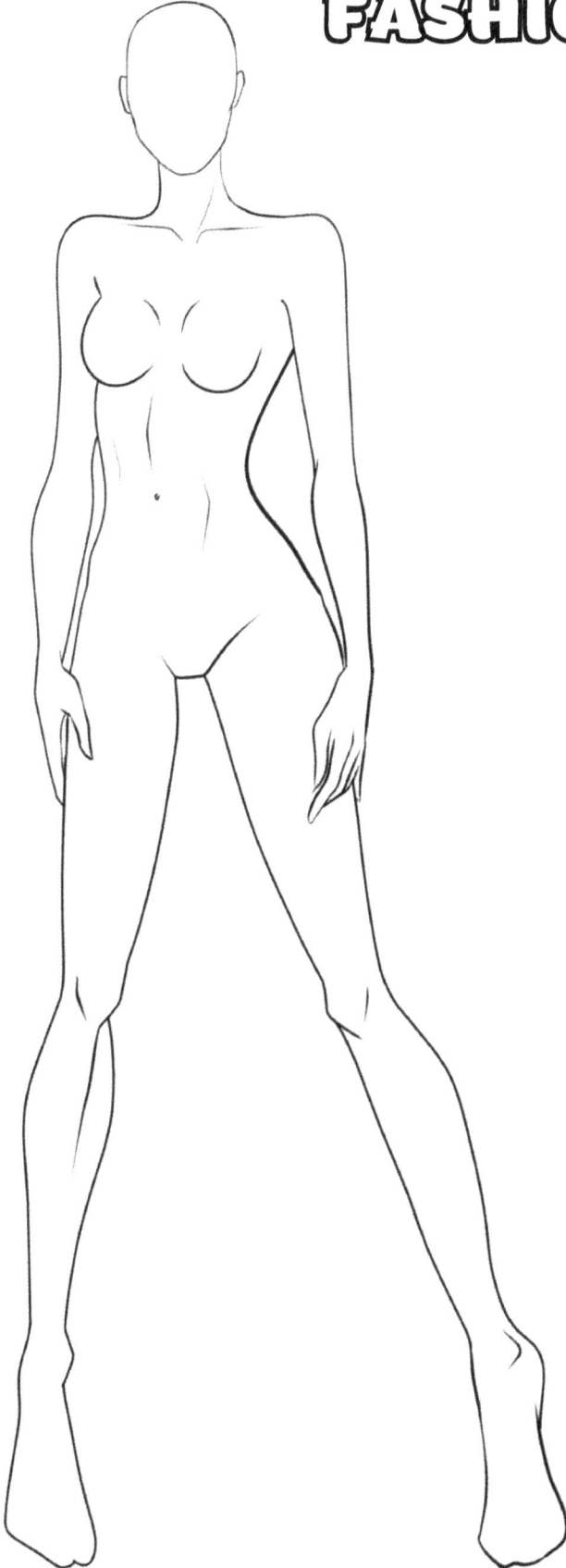

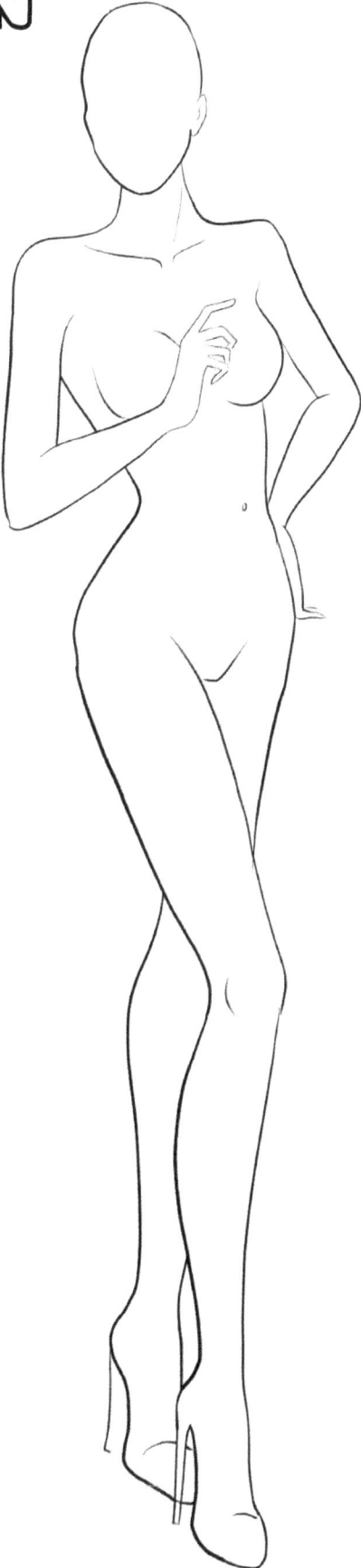

FASHION

FASHION

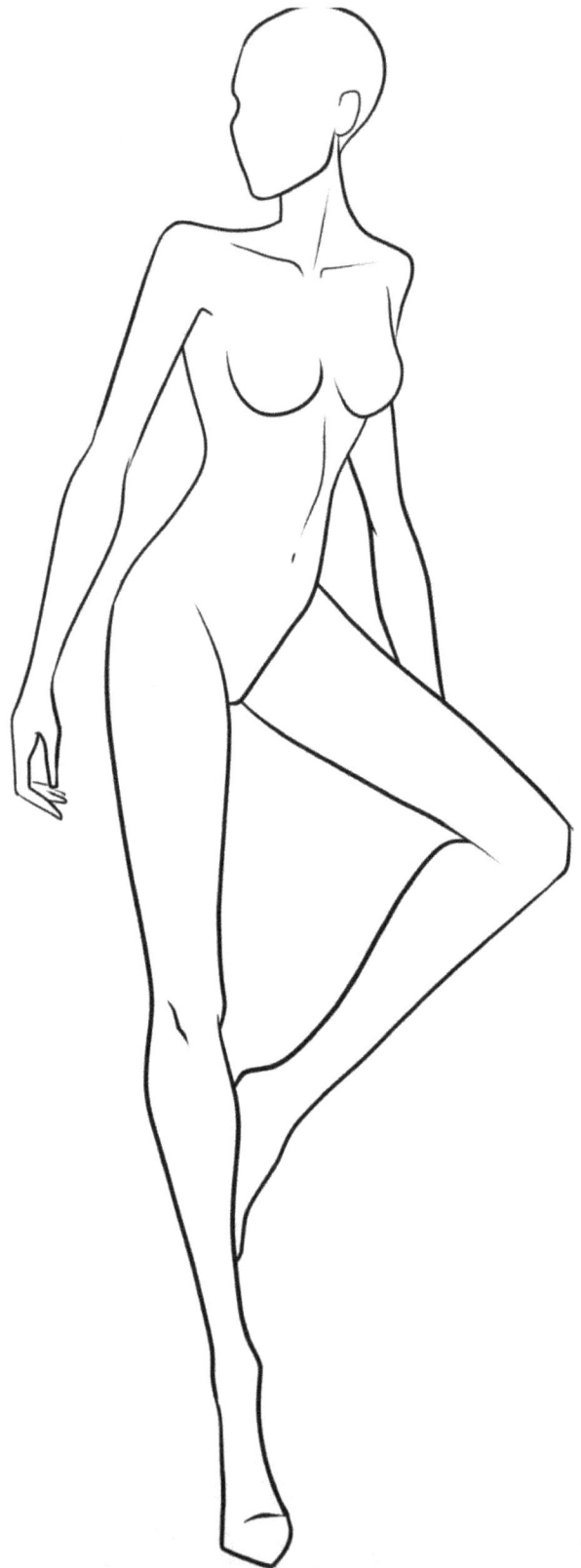

FASHION

FASHION

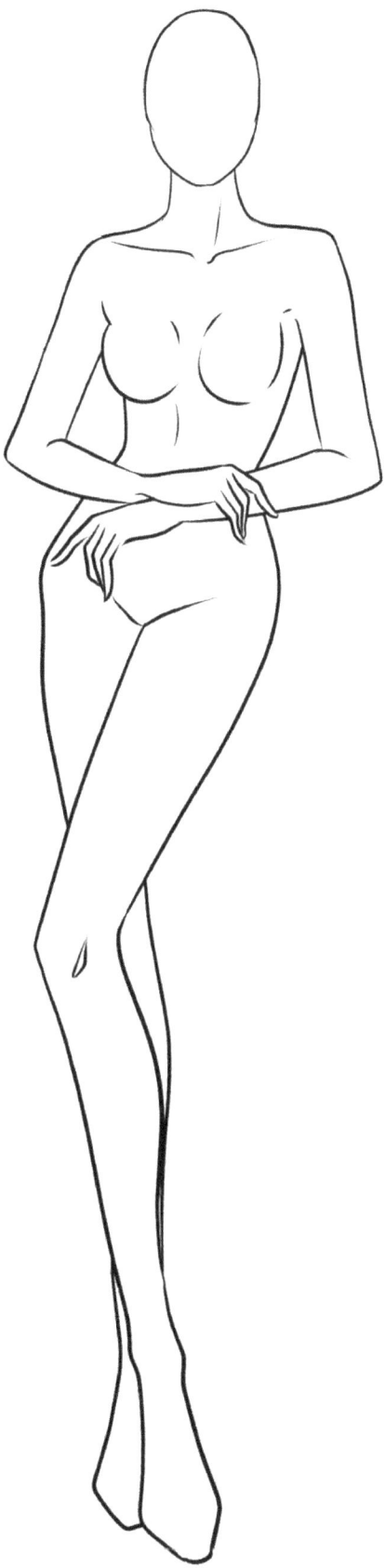

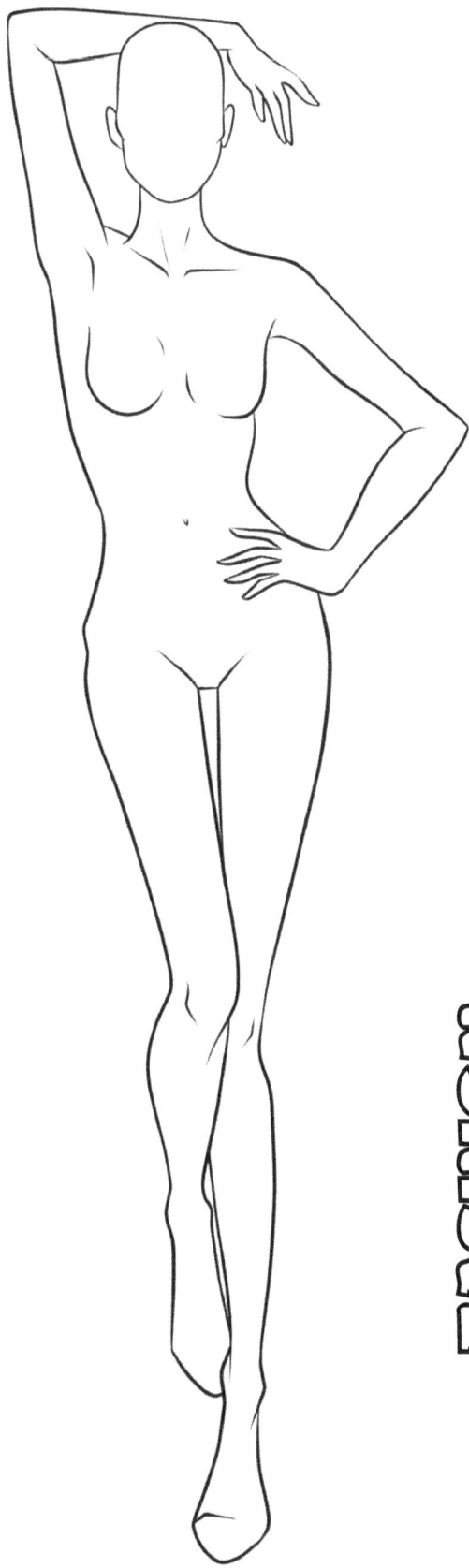

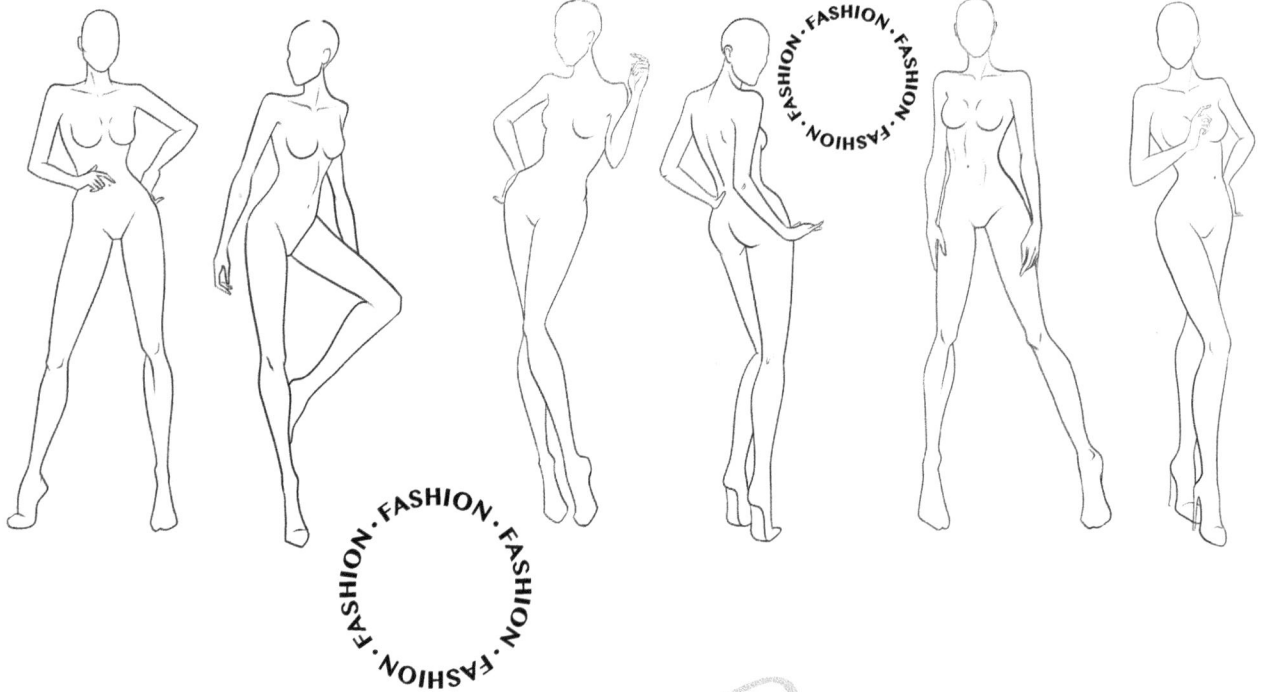

Niky Jadesson

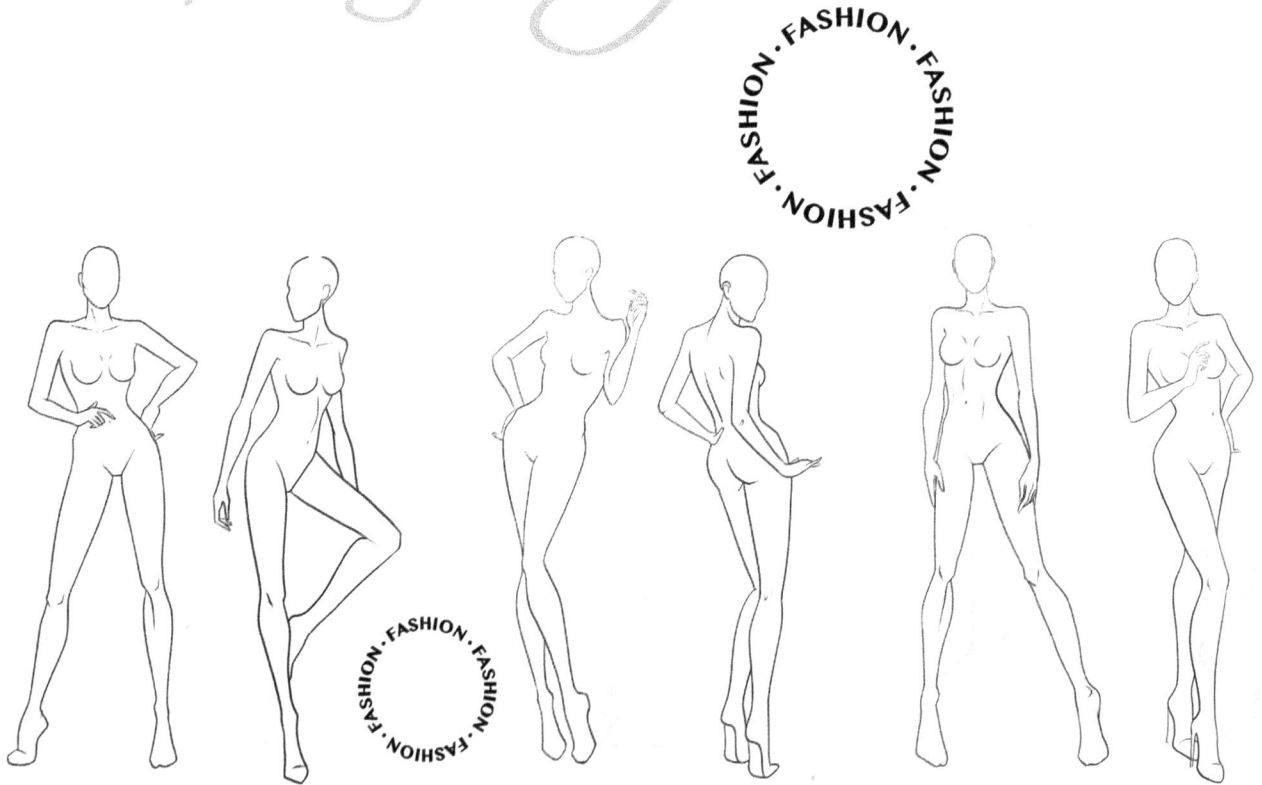

www.ingramcontent.com/pod-product-compliance
Lightning Source LLC
Chambersburg PA
CBHW080627030426
42336CB00018B/3106